The Original
# Summer Bridge Activities™

**4 to 5**

P9-DIY-721

*Teacher Recommended!*

Carson-Dellosa Publishing LLC
P.O. Box 35665 • Greensboro, NC 27425 USA

carsondellosa.com

*Caution*: Exercise activities may require adult supervision. Before beginning any exercise activity, consult a physician. Written parental permission is suggested for those using this book in group situations. Children should always warm up prior to beginning any exercise activity and should stop immediately if they feel any discomfort during exercise.

*Caution*: Before beginning any food activity, ask parents' permission and inquire about the child's food allergies and religious or other food restrictions.

*Caution*: Nature activities may require adult supervision. Before beginning any nature activity, ask parents' permission and inquire about the child's plant and animal allergies. Remind the child not to touch plants or animals during the activity without adult supervision.

The authors and publisher are not responsible or liable for any injury that may result from performing the exercises or activities in this book.

ISBN 978-1-62057-611-3

01-002131151

# Table of Contents

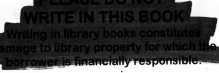

# About Summer Learning

Dear Parents:

Did you know that many children experience learning loss when they do not engage in educational activities during the summer? This means that some of what they have spent time learning over the preceding school year evaporates during the summer months. However, summer learning loss is something that you can help prevent. Below are a few suggestions for fun and engaging activities that can help children maintain and grow their academic skills during the summer.

- Read with your child every day. Visit your local library together and select books on subjects that interest your child.

- Ask your child's teacher to recommend books for summer reading.

- Explore parks, nature preserves, museums, and cultural centers.

- Consider every day as a day full of teachable moments. Measuring ingredients for recipes and reviewing maps before a car trip are ways to learn or reinforce skills.

- Each day, set goals for your child to accomplish. For example, complete five math problems or read one section or chapter in a book.

- Encourage your child to complete the activities in books such as Summer Bridge Activities™ to help bridge the summer learning gap.

To learn more about summer learning loss and summer learning programs, visit *www.summerlearning.org*.

Have a memorable summer!

Brenda McLaughlin and Sarah Pitcock
National Summer Learning Association

# About Summer Bridge Activities™

*Summer Bridge Activities™: Bridging Grades Fourth to Fifth* helps prepare your rising fifth grader for a successful school year. The activities in this book are designed to review the skills that your child mastered in fourth grade, preview the skills that he or she will learn in fifth grade, and help prevent summer learning loss. No matter how wonderful your child's classroom experiences are, your involvement outside of the classroom is crucial to his or her academic success. Together with *Summer Bridge Activities™: Bridging Grades Fourth to Fifth*, you can fill the summer months with learning experiences that will deepen and enrich your child's knowledge and prepare your child for the upcoming school year.

Summer Bridge Activities™ is the original workbook series developed to help parents support their children academically during the summer months. While many other summer workbook series are available, Summer Bridge Activities™ continues to be the series that teachers recommend most.

The three sections in this workbook correspond to the three months of traditional summer vacation. Each section begins with a goal-setting activity, a word list, and information about the fitness and character development activities located throughout the section.

To achieve maximum results, your child should complete two activity pages each day. Activities cover a range of subjects, including geometry, time and money, reading comprehension, vocabulary development, and writing. These age-appropriate activities are presented in a fun and creative way to challenge and engage your child. Each activity page is numbered by day, and each day includes a space for your child to place a colorful, motivational sticker after he or she completes the day's activities.

Bonus extension activities that encourage outdoor learning, science experiments, and social studies exercises are located at the end of each section. Complete these activities with your child throughout each month as time allows.

An answer key located at the end of the book allows you to check your child's work. The included flash cards help reinforce basic skills, and a certificate of completion will help you and your child celebrate his or her summer learning success!

# Skills Matrix

| Day | Addition | Data Analysis | Division | Fitness & Character Education | Fractions | Geometry | Grammar | Language Arts | Measurement | Mixed Math Practice | Multiplication | Puzzles | Reading Comprehension | Science | Social Studies | Subtraction | Time & Money | Vocabulary | Word Problems | Writing |
|---|---|---|---|---|---|---|---|---|---|---|---|---|---|---|---|---|---|---|---|---|
| 1 | | | | ★ | | | ★ | ★ | | ★ | | | | | | | | | | |
| 2 | | | | | | | ★ | | | ★ | | | ★ | | | | | | | |
| 3 | | | | | | | ★ | ★ | | ★ | | | | | | | ★ | | | |
| 4 | | | | | | ★ | | ★ | | | | | ★ | | | | | | | |
| 5 | | | | | | | ★ | | | ★ | | | | | | | | | | |
| 6 | | | | | | | ★ | ★ | | | | ★ | | | | | | | | |
| 7 | | | | | | | | | | ★ | | | ★ | | | | | | | ★ |
| 8 | | | ★ | | | | ★ | ★ | | | | | | | | | | | | |
| 9 | | | | | | | ★ | | | | | | ★ | | | | | ★ | | |
| 10 | | | | | | | ★ | | | | ★ | | | | ★ | | | | | |
| 11 | | | ★ | | | ★ | ★ | | | | | | | | | | | | | |
| 12 | ★ | | | | | | ★ | | | | | ★ | | | | | | | | |
| 13 | | | ★ | | | | | | | | | | ★ | | | | | | | |
| 14 | | | | | | ★ | ★ | | | | | | | | | | | | | |
| 15 | | | | | | | ★ | | | | | ★ | | | | ★ | | | | |
| 16 | | | | | | | ★ | | | ★ | | | | | | | | ★ | | |
| 17 | | | | | | | ★ | ★ | | | | | ★ | | | | | | | |
| 18 | | | | | | | ★ | | ★ | | | | | | | | | | | ★ |
| 19 | | | | | | | ★ | | | | | | ★ | | | | | ★ | ★ | |
| 20 | | | ★ | | | | | | | | | | | | ★ | | ★ | | | |
| **BONUS PAGES!** | | | | | | | | | | | | | | ★ | ★ | | | | | |
| 1 | | | | ★ | | | ★ | | | | | | | | | | | | | ★ |
| 2 | | | | | | | | ★ | | ★ | | | | | | ★ | | | | |
| 3 | | | | | | | ★ | | ★ | | ★ | | | | | | | | | |
| 4 | | | | | | | | ★ | | | | | ★ | | | | | | | ★ |
| 5 | | ★ | | | | | ★ | | | ★ | | | | | | | | | | |
| 6 | | | | | | | ★ | | | ★ | | ★ | | | | | | | | |
| 7 | | | | | | | ★ | ★ | | | | | | | | | | | | |
| 8 | | | ★ | | | | ★ | ★ | | | | | | | | | ★ | | | |
| 9 | | | ★ | | | | ★ | | | | | | | | | | | | | ★ |
| 10 | | | | | | | ★ | | | | | | | ★ | ★ | | | | | |
| 11 | | | | | ★ | | | | | | | | ★ | | | | | | | |

# Skills Matrix

| Day | Addition | Data Analysis | Division | Fitness & Character Education | Fractions | Geometry | Grammar | Language Arts | Measurement | Mixed Math Practice | Multiplication | Puzzles | Reading Comprehension | Science | Social Studies | Subtraction | Time & Money | Vocabulary | Word Problems | Writing |
|---|---|---|---|---|---|---|---|---|---|---|---|---|---|---|---|---|---|---|---|---|
| 12 | | | | | ★ | | ★ | | | | | | ★ | | | | | | | |
| 13 | | | | ★ | | | | ★ | | | ★ | ★ | | | | | | | | |
| 14 | | ★ | | | | | ★ | | | | | | | | | | | | | ★ |
| 15 | | | | | | ★ | ★ | | | | | | ★ | | | | | | | |
| 16 | | | | | | | ★ | ★ | | | | | | ★ | | | | | | |
| 17 | | | | | ★ | | | | | | | | ★ | | | | | ★ | | |
| 18 | | | | | | ★ | | ★ | | | | | | | | | | | | ★ |
| 19 | | | | | | | | ★ | | | | | | ★ | | | | | | ★ |
| 20 | | | | ★ | ★ | | | ★ | | | | | | | | | | | | ★ |
| | | | | | | | | BONUS PAGES! | | | | | | ★ | ★ | | | | | |
| 1 | | | | ★ | ★ | | | | | | | | ★ | | | | | | | |
| 2 | | | | | ★ | | ★ | | | | | ★ | | | | | | | | |
| 3 | | | | | | | | | ★ | | | | ★ | | | | | | | ★ |
| 4 | | | | | | | | ★ | | ★ | | | | ★ | | | | | | |
| 5 | | ★ | | | | | | | | | | | ★ | | | | | | | |
| 6 | | | | | | | | ★ | | | | | ★ | | | | | | | ★ |
| 7 | | | | | ★ | | ★ | ★ | | | | | | | | | | | | ★ |
| 8 | | | | | ★ | | ★ | | | | | | ★ | | | | | | | |
| 9 | | ★ | | | | ★ | ★ | | ★ | | | | | | | | | | | |
| 10 | | | | | | ★ | ★ | | | ★ | | | | | ★ | | | | | |
| 11 | | | | | | | ★ | | | ★ | | | ★ | | | | | | | |
| 12 | | | | | | | ★ | | ★ | | | | | | | | | | | |
| 13 | | | | | | | | ★ | | | | | ★ | | ★ | | | | | |
| 14 | | | ★ | | | | | | | | | | ★ | | | | | | | ★ |
| 15 | | | | | | ★ | ★ | | | | | | ★ | | | | | | | |
| 16 | | | | | | ★ | ★ | | | | | | | | | | | ★ | | |
| 17 | | | | ★ | ★ | | | | ★ | | | | | | | | | ★ | | |
| 18 | | ★ | | | | | | ★ | | | | | ★ | | | | | | | |
| 19 | | ★ | ★ | | | | | ★ | | | | | | | | | | | | |
| 20 | | | | | | | | | | | | | | ★ | ★ | | | | | |
| | | | ★ | | | | | BONUS PAGES! | | | | | | ★ | ★ | | | | | |

# Encouraging Summer Reading

Literacy is the single most important skill that your child needs to be successful in school. The following list includes ideas of ways that you can help your child discover the great adventures of reading!

- Establish a time for reading each day. Ask your child about what he or she is reading. Try to relate the material to an event that is happening this summer or to another book or story.

- Let your child see you reading for enjoyment. Talk about the great things that you discover when you read.

- Create a summer reading list. Choose books from the reading list (pages ix–x) or head to the library and explore the shelves. A general rule for selecting books at the appropriate reading level is to choose a page and ask your child to read it aloud. If he or she does not know more than five words on the page, the book may be too difficult.

- Read newspaper and magazine articles, recipes, menus, and maps on a daily basis to show your child the importance of reading.

- Find books that relate to your child's experiences. For example, if you are going camping, find a book about camping. This will help your child develop new interests.

- Visit the library each week. Let your child choose his or her own books, but do not hesitate to ask your librarian for suggestions. Often, librarians can recommend books based on what your child enjoyed in the past.

- Make up stories. This is especially fun to do in the car, on camping trips, or while waiting at the airport. Encourage your child to tell a story with a beginning, a middle, and an end. Or, have your child start a story and let other family members build on it.

- Encourage your child to join a summer reading club at the library or a local bookstore. Your child may enjoy talking to other children about the books that he or she has read.

# Summer Reading List

The summer reading list includes fiction and nonfiction titles. Experts recommend that fourth- and fifth-grade children read for at least 25 to 30 minutes each day. Then, ask questions about the story to reinforce comprehension.

Decide on an amount of daily reading time for each month. You may want to write the time on each Monthly Goals page at the beginning of each section.

## Fiction

Barshaw, Ruth McNally
*Ellie McDoodle: Have Pen, Will Travel*

Baum, L. Frank (adapted by Michael Cavallaro)
*L. Frank Baum's The Wizard of Oz: The Graphic Novel*

Blume, Judy
*Superfudge*

Cherry, Lynne and Mark J. Plotkin
*The Shaman's Apprentice: A Tale of the Amazon Rain Forest*

Christian, Mary Blount
*Sebastian (Super Sleuth) and the Copycat Crime*

Cleary, Beverly
*Henry and the Clubhouse*
*Henry Huggins*
*Ramona's World*
*Ribsy*

Collins, Suzanne
Underland Chronicles (series)

Dahl, Roald
*The BFG*
*Charlie and the Chocolate Factory*

Danziger, Paula
*There's a Bat in Bunk Five*

De Campi, Alex
*Agent Boo*

DeJong, Meindert
*The House of Sixty Fathers*

DiCamillo, Kate
*Because of Winn-Dixie*

du Bois, William Pène
*The Twenty-One Balloons*

Farber, Erica and Mayer, Mercer
*The Alien from Outer Space: A Graphic Novel Adventure*

Fox, Paula
*Maurice's Room*

Goble, Paul
*The Girl Who Loved Wild Horses*

Heard, Georgia (ed.)
*Falling Down the Page: A Book of List Poems*

Juster, Norton
*The Phantom Tollbooth*

Levine, Ellen
*Henry's Freedom Box: A True Story from the Underground Railroad*

Lewis, C. S.
*The Lion, the Witch and the Wardrobe*

Martin, Ann M.
*A Dog's Life: the Autobiography of a Stray*

# Summary Reading List (continued)

## Fiction (continued)

Morse, Scott
*Magic Pickle*

O'Brien, Robert C.
*Mrs. Frisby and the Rats of NIMH*

O'Dell, Scott
*Island of the Blue Dolphins*

O'Malley, Kevin
*Once Upon a Cool Motorcycle Dude*

Paulsen, Gary
*Lawn Boy*

Rowling, J. K.
*Harry Potter and the Sorcerer's Stone*

Rylant, Cynthia
*Missing May*

Sachar, Louis
*Sideways Stories from Wayside School*

Say, Allen
*Tea with Milk*

Silverstein, Shel
*Where the Sidewalk Ends*

Van Allsburg, Chris
*Jumanji*

Viorst, Judith
*Earrings!*

Waters, Kate
*Tapenum's Day: A Wampanoag Indian Boy in Pilgrim Times*

White, E. B.
*Charlotte's Web*
*Stuart Little*
*The Trumpet of the Swan*

Wilder, Laura Ingalls
*Little House on the Prairie*

## Nonfiction

Cherry, Lynne and Gary Braasch
*How We Know What We Know About Our Changing Climate: Scientists and Kids Explore Global Warming*

Colbert, David
*10 Days: Martin Luther King Jr.*

Dyer, Alan
*Mission to the Moon*

Nicklin, Flip and Linda
*Face to Face with Dolphins*

Pratt-Serafini, Kristin Joy and Rachel Crandell
*The Forever Forest: Kids Save a Tropical Treasure*

Robbins, Ken
*Thunder on the Plains: The Story of the American Buffalo*

Silverstein, Alvin and Virginia Silverstein
*Life in a Bucket of Soil*

Sís, Peter
*The Wall: Growing Up Behind the Iron Curtain*

Squire, Ann O.
*Growing Crystals*
*Rocks and Minerals*

St. George, Judith
*Sacajawea*
*So You Want to Be an Inventor?*

## Monthly Goals

A goal is something that you want to accomplish. Sometimes, reaching a goal can be hard work!

Think of three goals to set for yourself this month. For example, you may want to learn three new vocabulary words each week. Write your goals on the lines and review them with an adult.

Place a sticker next to each goal that you complete. Feel proud that you have met your goals!

1. _____    PLACE STICKER HERE

2. _____    PLACE STICKER HERE

3. _____    PLACE STICKER HERE

## Word List

The following words are used in this section. They are good words for you to know. Read each word aloud. Use a dictionary to look up each word that you do not know. Then, write two sentences. Use a word from the word list in each sentence.

admire                    healthy
energy                    knowledge
geometry                  leader
government                passage

1. _____

_____

2. _____

_____

# Introduction to Flexibility

This section includes fitness and character development activities that focus on flexibility. These activities are designed to get you moving and thinking about building your physical fitness and your character.

## Physical Flexibility

For many people, being flexible means easily doing everyday tasks, such as bending to tie a shoe. Tasks like this can be hard for people who do not stretch often. Stretching will make your muscles more flexible. It can also improve your balance and coordination.

You probably stretch every day without realizing it. Do you ever reach for a dropped pencil or a box of cereal on the top shelf? If you do, then you are stretching. Try to improve your flexibility this summer. Set a stretching goal. For example, you might stretch every day until you can touch your toes.

## Flexibility of Character

It is good to have a flexible body. It is also good to be mentally flexible. This means being open to change.

It can be upsetting when things do not go your way. Can you think of a time when an unexpected event ruined your plans? For example, a family trip to the zoo was canceled because the car had a flat tire. Unexpected events happen sometimes. How you react to those events often affects the outcome. Arm yourself with the tools to be flexible. Have realistic expectations. Find ways to make the situation better. Look for good things that may have come from the event.

You can be mentally flexible by showing respect to other people. Sharing and taking turns are also ways to be mentally flexible. This character trait gets easier with practice. Over the summer, practice and use your mental flexibility often.

**Solve each problem.**

1.  $13 - 5 = $ _____

2.  $15 - 9 = $ _____

3.  $4 \times 3 = $ _____

4.  $9 + 2 = $ _____

5.  $10 \div 2 = $ _____

6.  $6 + 4 = $ _____

7.  $6 \times 5 = $ _____

8.  $30 \div 6 = $ _____

9.  $13 + 5 = $ _____

10.  $17 - 9 = $ _____

11.  $3 \times 6 = $ _____

12.  $27 \div 3 = $ _____

**Find each missing number.**

13.  $18 \div \boxed{\phantom{0}} = 6$

14.  $4 \times \boxed{\phantom{0}} = 36$

15.  $\boxed{\phantom{0}} - 6 = 7$

16.  $\boxed{\phantom{0}} + 6 = 12$

17.  $10 - \boxed{\phantom{0}} = 3$

18.  $24 \div \boxed{\phantom{0}} = 3$

19.  $3 \times \boxed{\phantom{0}} = 21$

20.  $\boxed{\phantom{0}} \div 6 = 4$

21.  $\boxed{\phantom{0}} \times 7 = 0$

**A sentence is a group of words that expresses a complete thought. Write *yes* before each group of words if it is a sentence. Write *no* if the group is not a sentence.**

22.  _____ Tom bought the food.

23.  _____ Turtles have hard shells.

24.  _____ Will you feed the pets?

25.  _____ We will turn to page.

26.  _____ Butterflies beautiful.

27.  _____ They enjoyed the trip.

28.  _____ Don't forget to call me!

29.  _____ Ants are insects.

30.  _____ For his 10th birthday.

31.  _____ Puppies fun!

32.  _____ Wrapped the gift.

33.  _____ Vacation nice.

# DAY 1

**A thesaurus is a reference book that contains synonyms and antonyms. In each row, circle the word that does not belong.**

| | | | | |
|---|---|---|---|---|
| 34. | family | tribe | clan | enemy |
| 35. | time | Earth | globe | sphere |
| 36. | notice | overlook | observe | see |
| 37. | sky | sun | orb | planet |

## Stretch Your Limits

If you are going to a pool, a beach, or a lake to cool off this summer, try doing a post-swimming stretch called the cobra stretch. Lie on your stomach with your legs stretched behind you. The soles of your feet should be facing up. Place your hands on the ground under your shoulders. Keep your elbows close to your body. As you take a deep breath, push your hands into the ground and lift your chest as high as is comfortable. Relax and look up slightly, stretching your lower back and breathing easily. Hold the stretch for 20 seconds.

**FACTOID:** Ladybugs chew their food from side to side, not up and down.

* See page ii.

PLACE STICKER HERE

**Use each fact family to create number sentences.**

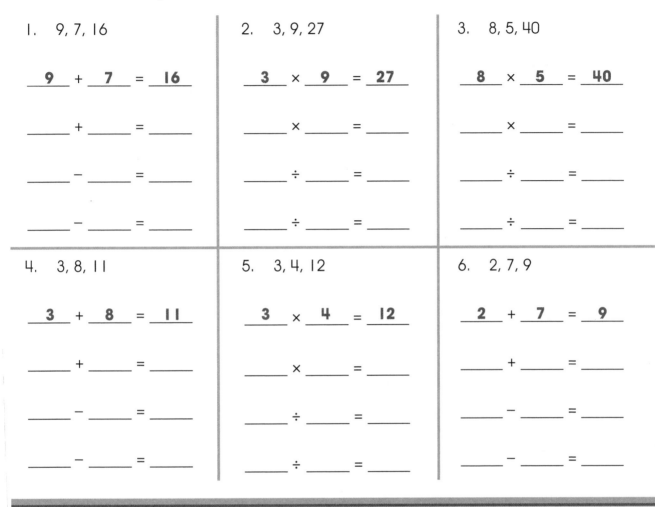

1.  9, 7, 16

   __9__ + __7__ = __16__

   _____ + _____ = _____

   _____ − _____ = _____

   _____ − _____ = _____

2.  3, 9, 27

   __3__ × __9__ = __27__

   _____ × _____ = _____

   _____ ÷ _____ = _____

   _____ ÷ _____ = _____

3.  8, 5, 40

   __8__ × __5__ = __40__

   _____ × _____ = _____

   _____ ÷ _____ = _____

   _____ ÷ _____ = _____

4.  3, 8, 11

   __3__ + __8__ = __11__

   _____ + _____ = _____

   _____ − _____ = _____

   _____ − _____ = _____

5.  3, 4, 12

   __3__ × __4__ = __12__

   _____ × _____ = _____

   _____ ÷ _____ = _____

   _____ ÷ _____ = _____

6.  2, 7, 9

   __2__ + __7__ = __9__

   _____ + _____ = _____

   _____ − _____ = _____

   _____ − _____ = _____

**Draw a line to connect each word to its abbreviation.**

7.  Sunday        ex.

8.  quart         Sun.

9.  ounce         oz.

10. example       qt.

11. Friday        Fri.

12. pound         pt.

13. pint          lb.

14. October       Oct.

# DAY 2

**Read the passage. Then, answer the questions.**

## Giant Sequoias

The first giant sequoia trees probably started growing in North America about 180 million years ago. Giant sequoia trees can live more than 3,000 years. For the first 250 years, giant sequoias look like small pine trees. Giant sequoias reach their full height when they are about 500 years old. The giant sequoia can grow as tall as a 25-story building—that's about 250 feet (76 m) tall! Some trees have grown up to 30 feet (9 m) wide, or as wide as a three-lane highway. The largest giant sequoia living today is named General Sherman. General Sherman is over 274 feet (83 m) tall.

There are not many sequoias alive today. Millions of years ago, sequoias grew across North America. Then, the weather turned colder. These trees needed the warm weather to live. Now, when people visit the remaining sequoia forests, they drive and walk over the ground. This makes the ground hard. The sequoias' roots have a difficult time absorbing water in the hard ground. This is killing some of the trees. However, some people take home seeds when they visit the sequoia forests. They plant the seeds all over the world. Someday, these seeds may develop into new forests.

15. How long does it take a giant sequoia tree to reach its full height?_____

16. How tall is the largest giant sequoia tree living today?_____

17. Why are fewer giant sequoias alive today than in the past? _____

_____

_____

18. What are two things that giant sequoias need in order to survive?_____

_____

**FITNESS FLASH:** Practice a V-sit. Stretch five times.

* See page ii.

PLACE STICKER HERE

**When estimating numbers, round each number to the nearest place value before adding or subtracting. Estimate the sums and differences.**

**EXAMPLE:**

| | | |
|---|---|---|
| 81 + 75 ≈ <br><br> __80__ + __80__ = __160__ | 1. 93 − 12 ≈ <br><br> _____ − _____ = _____ | 2. 98 − 12 ≈ <br><br> _____ − _____ = _____ |
| 3. 93 − 39 ≈ <br><br> _____ − _____ = _____ | 4. 891 − 551 ≈ <br><br> _____ − _____ = _____ | 5. 57 − 39 ≈ <br><br> _____ − _____ = _____ |
| 6. 24 + 35 ≈ <br><br> _____ + _____ = _____ | 7. 209 + 179 ≈ <br><br> _____ + _____ = _____ | 8. 64 + 39 ≈ <br><br> _____ + _____ = _____ |

**A common noun names any person, place, or thing. A proper noun names a particular person, place, or thing. Circle each common noun and underline each proper noun.**

9. Christopher Columbus was an explorer.

10. Antarctica is a continent.

11. We paddled the canoe down the Red River.

12. Fido is my favorite dog.

13. San Francisco is the city by the bay.

14. She visited her aunt in Boston.

15. Mount Mitchell is a mountain.

16. Thursday is my birthday.

## DAY 3

There are 24 hours in a day. The times from midnight through 11:59 in the morning are written A.M., and the times from noon through 11:59 at night are written P.M. Write the correct times.

A.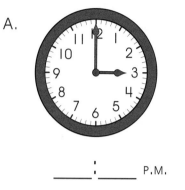

_____:_____ P.M.

B.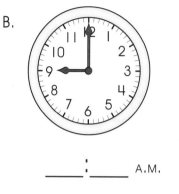

_____:_____ A.M.

C.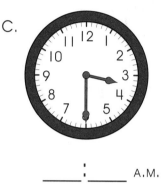

_____:_____ A.M.

17. 50 minutes later than clock A

_____

18. If you add 12 hours to clock A, what time is it? _____

19. 25 minutes earlier than clock B

_____

20. What was the time 6 hours earlier than clock B? _____

21. 95 minutes later than clock C

_____

22. How much earlier is clock C than clock B? _____

---

**Write as many smaller words as possible from the letters in each word.**

**EXAMPLE:** borrow _____*bow*_____ _____*row*_____ _____*brow*_____

23. pajamas _____

24. tomorrow _____

25. performance _____

**FACTOID:** A mermaid's purse is a case of eggs laid by a shark or ray in the ocean.

PLACE STICKER HERE

**Use what you know about polygons to make a pattern. Start with one polygon, and flip, turn, or slide it to make a pattern.**

EXAMPLE:

---

**Rewrite this address correctly.**

1461 condor st

mr greg jones

lake tona oh

98562

**Read the passage. Then, answer the questions.**

## Astronomers

Astronomy is the study of planets, stars, and the universe. The first astronomers were ancient people who observed star patterns called constellations. They gave them names, such as the Great Bear. Today, astronomers seek to learn about the universe. They use powerful telescopes to see stars and to measure their distance from Earth and the speed at which they are moving. Astronomers interpret data collected by satellites and spacecrafts. By using readings from different instruments, astronomers can predict when objects such as comets and meteors will appear in the night sky. Sometimes, astronomers discover new things in outer space. Halley's Comet, which can be seen every 76 years, was named after Edmond Halley, the astronomer who predicted that the comet would return in 1758. The names of modern astronomical discoveries must be approved by the International Astronomical Union, a professional organization for astronomers.

1. What is the main idea of this passage?

   a. Astronomers look at constellations of stars.

   b. Astronomers study objects in outer space.

   c. Some astronomers discover new comets.

2. What is astronomy?_____

3. Why do astronomers use telescopes?_____

   _____

4. What do astronomers try to predict using different instruments? _____

   _____

5. How did Halley's Comet get its name? _____

   _____

**FITNESS FLASH: Touch your toes 10 times.**

* See page ii.

PLACE STICKER HERE

1.  **Underline each noun that names a person.**

    | | | | |
    |---|---|---|---|
    | boy | house | table | game |
    | coach | friend | sister | teacher |
    | doctor | assistant | student | actor |

2.  **Underline each noun that names a place.**

    | | | | |
    |---|---|---|---|
    | laboratory | park | paper | clinic |
    | playground | classroom | dog | office |
    | sun | hallway | food | diner |

3.  **Underline each noun that names a thing.**

    | | | | |
    |---|---|---|---|
    | desk | truck | window | city |
    | neighbor | dictionary | banana | book |
    | house | lunch box | ruler | teacher |

**Answer each question.**

4.  In a newspaper or magazine, find and circle three numbers. Write each number in word form, standard form, and expanded form.

    _____

    _____

5.  Write a few sentences about the important role that numbers play in your daily life. Why is it important to be able to recognize the same number written in different forms?

    _____

    _____

    _____

# DAY 5

**Solve each problem.**

6.     681
     + 145

7.     428
     − 119

8.     4,918
     + 3,928

9.     248
     + 48

10.     569
     − 247

11.     2,709
     + 1,282

12.     304
     − 172

13.     143
     + 219

---

The word *their* shows ownership, and the word *there* shows a place. Complete each sentence with *their* or *there*.

14.   I left my coat _____ yesterday.

15.   Ian and Mackenzie were training _____ horses to jump.

16.   We are going to _____ farm tomorrow.

17.   Please put the box over_____ .

18.   Will you please sit here, not _____ ?

**Write two sentences about your school. Use *their* in one sentence and *there* in the other.**

19.   _____

20.   _____

**CHARACTER CHECK:** Think of a time when you did something nice for a friend or family member. How did that make you feel?

PLACE STICKER HERE

A suffix is added to the end of a base word. When some suffixes are added, it is necessary to double the base word's final consonant or change *y* to *i*. Add the suffix *-est* to the end of each base word and write the new word.

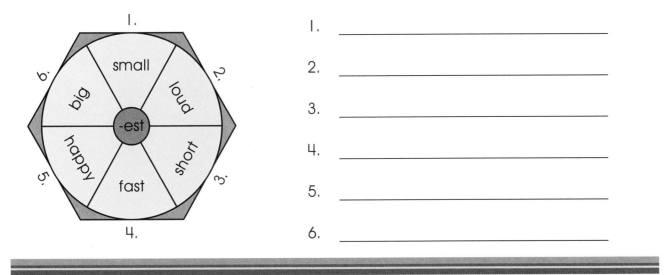

1. _____

2. _____

3. _____

4. _____

5. _____

6. _____

Homophones are words that sound the same but are spelled differently. Write five sentences. Use a pair of homophones from the word bank in each sentence. Underline the homophones.

| | | | |
|---|---|---|---|
| no, know | sun, son | tail, tale | new, knew |
| way, weigh | sent, cent | sale, sail | their, there |
| ate, eight | see, sea | pair, pear | blew, blue |

**EXAMPLE:**

*Would you chop some wood?*

7. _____

8. _____

9. _____

10. _____

11. _____

# DAY 6

## And the Winner Is . . .

In the United States, Election Day—the day citizens vote for public officials—is held on the first Tuesday after the first Monday in November. National elections throughout the country are also held on this day.

**Draw a line through the letters of each election word hidden in the puzzle. Letters can go across, backward, up, and down.**

| citizen | representative | national |
|---------|----------------|----------|
| Constitution | governor | ~~president~~ |
| senator | mayor | |

```
p  r  o  v  e  c  o  r  r  e
s  e  g  t  r  r  n  o  y  p
t  d  e  h  n  o  s  m  a  r
z  m  y  b  e  i  t  n  o  e
n  t  r  w  v  t  u  t  i  s
e  s  e  v  i  t  a  t  n  e
n  a  i  z  p  e  r  i  e  n
o  t  t  e  a  t  w  y  e  c
r  c  i  n  n  i  o  n  a  l
```

**FACTOID:** There are more than 950 species of bats in the world.

**Write the number for each letter on the number line.**

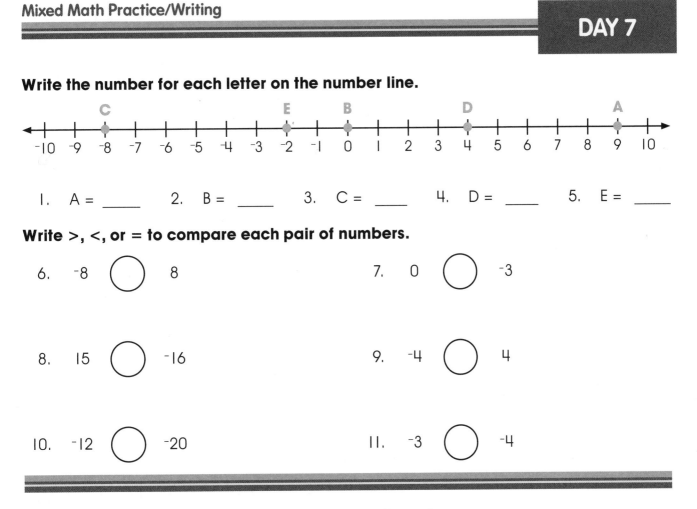

1.  A = ____    2.  B = ____    3.  C = ____    4.  D = ____    5.  E = ____

**Write >, <, or = to compare each pair of numbers.**

6.  ⁻8  ◯  8

7.  0  ◯  ⁻3

8.  15  ◯  ⁻16

9.  ⁻4  ◯  4

10.  ⁻12  ◯  ⁻20

11.  ⁻3  ◯  ⁻4

**Read the five steps of the writing process to write a story.**

A.  Plan

B.  First draft

C.  Revise

D.  Proofread

E.  Final draft

**Use the steps to finish the story on a separate sheet of paper.**

You go for a walk one day and find a large, golden egg with green spots. Suddenly, it begins to shake and crack.

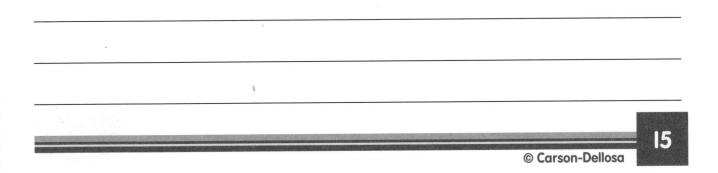

**Read the passage. Then, answer the questions.**

## Reptiles and Amphibians

You may think that lizards and frogs are in the same family, but they are not. Lizards, snakes, turtles, and crocodiles are reptiles. Frogs, toads, and salamanders are amphibians. Both amphibians and reptiles are cold-blooded, which means that the warmth of their bodies depends on their surroundings. Most reptiles and amphibians lay eggs instead of giving birth to their young. Reptiles lay hard-shelled eggs on land, but amphibians lay soft-shelled eggs in the water. When reptiles hatch, they look like tiny adults. Amphibian babies, such as tadpoles or baby frogs, must live underwater until they are older. Adult amphibians spend part of their time in the water and part on land. Reptiles feel dry and scaly to the touch, and amphibians feel moist and sticky. Because amphibians can live both in water and on land, they are more at risk for becoming sick from pollution. It is important to keep ponds and lakes clean so that the animals that live there will be safe and healthy.

12.  What is the main idea of this passage?

    a.   There are important differences between reptiles and amphibians.

    b.   Reptiles are the same as amphibians.

    c.   Frogs and lizards belong to different families.

13.  Name three animals that are reptiles._____

    _____

14.  Name three animals that are amphibians. _____

    _____

15.  How are amphibians and reptiles similar? _____

    _____

**FITNESS FLASH:** Do arm circles for 30 seconds.

* See page ii.

PLACE STICKER HERE

**Divide to find each quotient.**

1. 20 ÷ 4 = _____
2. 28 ÷ 4 = _____
3. 14 ÷ 7 = _____

4. 0 ÷ 2 = _____
5. 42 ÷ 6 = _____
6. 30 ÷ 5 = _____

7. 32 ÷ 4 = _____
8. 25 ÷ 5 = _____
9. 81 ÷ 9 = _____

10. 49 ÷ 7 = _____
11. 18 ÷ 6 = _____
12. 63 ÷ 7 = _____

13. 40 ÷ 5 = _____
14. 36 ÷ 9 = _____
15. 72 ÷ 9 = _____

16. 54 ÷ 6 = _____
17. 48 ÷ 6 = _____
18. 32 ÷ 8 = _____

19. 45 ÷ 9 = _____
20. 36 ÷ 6 = _____
21. 54 ÷ 9 = _____

**Helping verbs help the main verb. The main verb shows the action. In each sentence, underline the main verb and circle the helping verb.**

**EXAMPLE:** It (has been) raining for five days.

22. Jack had finished his lessons before 10:00.

23. I have enjoyed playing with my friends today.

24. We were cleaning the house for our friend.

25. The babies have been sleeping for two hours.

**Write a helping verb to complete each sentence.**

26. Uma _____ diving into the pond.

27. The pool _____ used all summer.

28. I _____ waiting for them to fix it.

29. They _____ working on it for three weeks.

# DAY 8

**A prefix is added to the beginning of a base word. Add a prefix to the base word in each sentence.**

30. The _____ game practice always comes before the game.

31. Do you agree or _____ agree with what I said?

32. Mother is going to _____ arrange the room one more time.

33. The three connected lines make a _____ angle.

34. Everyone on the team wears the same _____ form to the game.

35. You can count on me to _____ pay the money I borrowed.

36. He has to _____ tie his shoelaces to take off his shoes.

37. A _____ cycle has two wheels.

---

**A metaphor is a comparison between two objects that does not use the words *like* or *as*. Metaphors can make your writing more descriptive.**

**EXAMPLE:** Mika is a fish in the swimming pool. Mika swims well.

**Read the sentences. Then, write what each metaphor means.**

38. Your smile is a ray of sunshine. _____

39. Winning the award was a dream come true. _____

40. This store is a maze to walk through. _____

41. My pillow was a fluffy cloud. _____

**FACTOID:** Global temperatures have risen 1.4°F (0.8°C) since 1880.

PLACE
STICKER
HERE

**Solve each word problem.**

1.  Cammie has 3 coins worth 11¢. What are the coins?

    _____

2.  Troy has 7 coins worth 20¢. What are the coins?

    _____

3.  Janet has 6 coins worth 47¢. What are the coins?

    _____

4.  Jake has 4 coins worth 45¢. What are the coins?

    _____

5.  Frankie has 5 coins worth 17¢. What are the coins?

    _____

6.  Gary has 6 coins worth 40¢. What are the coins?

    _____

**A singular noun is one of something. A plural noun is more than one. Write the singular or plural form of each noun.**

**EXAMPLE:**  bee __*bees*__    boys __*boy*__

7.  bunny _____

8.  movie _____

9.  windows _____

10.  branch _____

11.  cities _____

12.  goose _____

13.  child _____

14.  foot _____

15.  toe _____

16.  boxes _____

17.  libraries _____

18.  men _____

19.  buses _____

20.  class _____

# DAY 9

**Read the passage. Then, answer the questions.**

## The Continents

The earth is divided into seven large areas of land called continents. The seven continents are Asia, Africa, Australia, Europe, Antarctica, North America, and South America. Each continent is separated from the others by either a body of water or a mountain range. Continents can be divided into countries, states, and provinces. Six of the seven continents are inhabited by people. Antarctica is at the south pole, where the weather is too cold for people to live year-round. However, some scientists live in special stations in Antarctica for part of the year to do research. The smallest continent is Australia, which covers nearly 3 million square miles (7.7 million km$^2$). The largest continent is Asia, which covers more than 17 million square miles (44 million km$^2$). Asia, with a population of more than 3 billion, has the most people living in it. That is about half of the world's population!

21. What is the main idea of this passage?

    a. More people live in Asia than in any other continent in the world.

    b. It is hard for people to live in Antarctica.

    c. Continents are large areas of land on the earth.

22. List the seven continents. _____

_____

_____

23. What is a station in Antarctica?

    a. a place where scientists study

    b. an area of the classroom

    c. a TV channel

24. About how much bigger is Asia than Australia? _____

**FITNESS FLASH:** Do 10 shoulder shrugs.

\* See page ii.

PLACE STICKER HERE

**Pronouns take the place of nouns. Write the pronoun that replaces each word or set of words in parentheses.**

Blair and Denise were best friends. (Blair and Denise) _____ decided to take a trip together. With maps and brochures scattered all over the floor, (Blair and Denise) _____ started looking for a place to visit. One brochure was especially interesting. (The brochure) _____ was about Yellowstone National Park. "Let's go see (Yellowstone) _____ !" said Denise.

"I think we should ask my brother Tom to go with us," said Blair. "(My brother) _____ could do some of the driving for _____ (Blair and Denise)."

The next day, Tom's car was packed and ready to go. (Blair, Denise, and Tom) _____ would have taken Blair's car, but (Blair's car) _____ had a flat tire. After driving for two days, the travelers arrived at Yellowstone National Park. Tom shouted, "At last we have arrived!" (Tom) _____ was tired of driving. (The trip) _____ turned out to be a lot of fun for (Blair, Denise, and Tom) _____ .

**Multiply to find each product.**

1. 9 × 2 = _____
2. 1 × 9 = _____
3. 7 × 9 = _____
4. 8 × 4 = _____
5. 4 × 7 = _____
6. 9 × 9 = _____
7. 5 × 6 = _____
8. 8 × 3 = _____
9. 8 × 5 = _____
10. 7 × 3 = _____
11. 3 × 3 = _____
12. 3 × 4 = _____
13. 4 × 6 = _____
14. 6 × 3 = _____
15. 5 × 5 = _____
16. 9 × 5 = _____
17. 6 × 9 = _____
18. 8 × 7 = _____
19. 8 × 8 = _____
20. 3 × 9 = _____
21. 7 × 7 = _____

# DAY 10

**Friendship Day is the first Sunday in August. Finish each sentence. Then, draw a picture to show what friendship means to you.**

Friends should always _____.

Friends should never _____.

I am a good friend because _____.

---

**An action verb tells what someone or something is doing. Circle the action verb in each sentence.**

**EXAMPLE:** The mouse scampers across the floor.

22. Oliver hides from his friend.

23. Fiona dashes behind the tree.

24. Marshall searches for the others.

25. Shauna sits under the swing.

26. Jane kneels behind the slide.

27. Drew crawls along the fence.

28. Emily races for the free spot.

29. Caleb finds Karen.

**CHARACTER CHECK:** Look up the word *considerate* in a dictionary. Then, think of two ways that you can be considerate.

PLACE STICKER HERE

**Parallel lines never meet. Draw a line that is parallel to each line segment.**

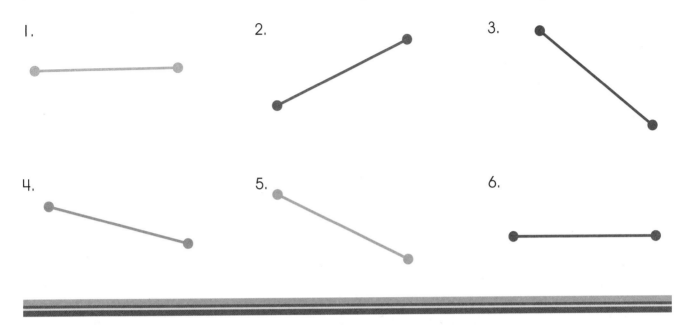

1.

2.

3.

4.

5.

6.

**A proper noun starts with a capital letter. Write a proper noun for each common noun.**

**EXAMPLE:** building *White House*

7. restaurant_____

8. person_____

9. holiday_____

10. country_____

11. national park_____

12. day_____

13. state_____

14. island_____

15. river_____

16. street_____

**Write a common noun for each proper noun.**

17. Golden Gate Bridge_____

18. Canada_____

19. San Francisco_____

20. Joseph_____

21. Pacific_____

22. Liberty Bell_____

23. November_____

24. Jamal_____

# DAY 11

**Divide to find each quotient.**

25. 4)28    26. 5)40    27. 7)49    28. 6)30

29. 8)72    30. 9)45    31. 8)32    32. 3)15

33. 7)56    34. 6)24    35. 7)14    36. 6)54

37. 9)9    38. 7)28    39. 6)42    40. 8)56

41. 7)35    42. 6)48    43. 9)81    44. 8)24

**Write the past tense of each verb in parentheses.**

45. Jarvis _____ he wanted to stay in touch with Kit. (know)

46. Nicole _____a letter to Ron. (write)

47. He_____his friend with him. (bring)

48. The workers _____ to dig the ditch. (begin)

49. That little girl_____ flowers again. (grow)

**FACTOID:** A shark can grow a new tooth in 24 hours.

PLACE STICKER HERE

**Add to find each sum.**

| | | | |
|---|---|---|---|
| 1.   2,456 <br> + 1,527 | 2.   9,873 <br> + 1,828 | 3.   18,086 <br> + 12,302 | 4.   21,421 <br> + 10,310 |
| 5.   19,873 <br> + 1,828 | 6.   8,024 <br> 3,643 <br> +   626 | 7.   4,877 <br> 3,481 <br> +   309 | 8.   5,221 <br> 4,708 <br> +   425 |

**A singular noun shows possession by adding 's to the end of the word. Most plural nouns show possession by adding only ' to the end. Complete each sentence with a singular or plural possessive noun from the word bank.**

| birds' | child's | dog's | cows' | sun's | shirt's |
|---|---|---|---|---|---|

9. The _____ rays are warm and bright.

10. The _____ favorite game is on the floor.

11. My _____ button fell off.

12. My _____ leash is black.

13. The _____ mooing was loud.

14. The _____ nests were high up in the trees.

# DAY 12

## There's No Comparison

**Write >, <, or = to compare each pair of numbers. Circle the letter next to the greater number. If the numbers are equal, circle both letters. To solve the riddle, write the circled letters in order on the lines.**

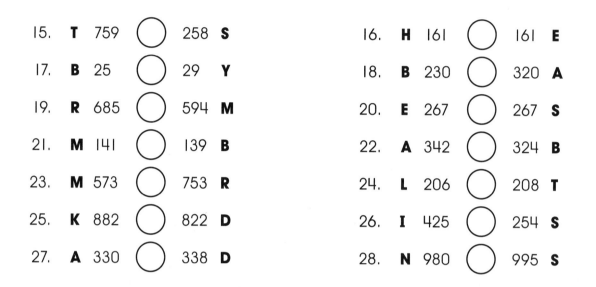

15. **T** 759 ◯ 258 **S**

16. **H** 161 ◯ 161 **E**

17. **B** 25 ◯ 29 **Y**

18. **B** 230 ◯ 320 **A**

19. **R** 685 ◯ 594 **M**

20. **E** 267 ◯ 267 **S**

21. **M** 141 ◯ 139 **B**

22. **A** 342 ◯ 324 **B**

23. **M** 573 ◯ 753 **R**

24. **L** 206 ◯ 208 **T**

25. **K** 882 ◯ 822 **D**

26. **I** 425 ◯ 254 **S**

27. **A** 330 ◯ 338 **D**

28. **N** 980 ◯ 995 **S**

**Why do baby goats know how to compare numbers?**

BECAUSE ____ ____ ____ ____    ____ ____ ____

____ ____ ____ ____    " ____ ____ ____ ____ "!

**FITNESS FLASH:** Practice a V-sit. Stretch five times.

\* See page ii.

PLACE STICKER HERE

## Sharing Stories

Respect means having consideration for someone else's feelings, possessions, and ideas. By now, you have had many opportunities to learn and show respect. Show your understanding of this key character trait by writing a story for younger children that demonstrates respect. Use a personal example from when you were younger and were learning about respect. After writing your story, design a cover to enclose the pages. Share your story with a younger family member or a family friend to help her learn about this important character trait. Use the space below to plan your story.

_____

_____

_____

_____

_____

_____

_____

_____

_____

_____

_____

_____

**Read the passage. Then, answer the questions.**

### Democracy

Democracy is a form of government in which people vote for the leaders who govern them. *Democracy* is derived from a Greek word meaning "popular government." Here, the word *popular* means "of the people" rather than "well liked." The word was first used to describe the political system of Greek city-states, like Athens, in the fourth and fifth centuries BC. In a direct democracy, the people vote on every decision. An example of a direct democracy is a club in which all members vote on decisions such as a poster design or how to raise money. It is hard for large groups to have a direct democracy, so many places, including the United States and Canada, have a representative democracy. In a representative democracy, people elect leaders who vote on the issues. The people trust that their elected leaders will represent their viewpoints. If the people feel that their elected leaders do not represent their viewpoints, then they can vote them out of office.

1. What is the main idea of this passage?

    a. Democracy is a form of government in which people make the decisions.

    b. An early form of democracy was practiced in Greece.

    c. The United States and Canada both have democratic governments.

2. What does the Greek word for *democracy* mean?_____

    _____

3. What happens in a direct democracy?_____

    _____

4. What happens in a representative democracy? _____

    _____

**FACTOID:** The largest frog in the world is the goliath frog, which can grow to a length of about one foot (about 30 cm).

**Write the contraction for each word pair in the circles to complete the puzzle.**

**EXAMPLE:** I would

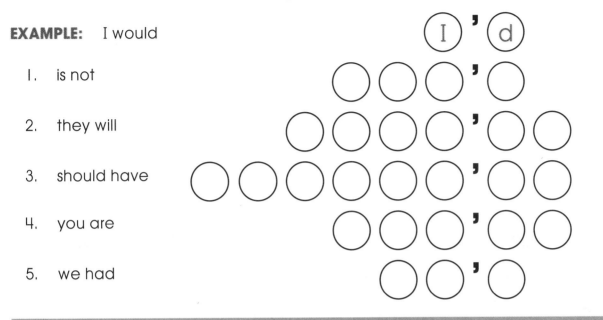

1. is not

2. they will

3. should have

4. you are

5. we had

**Follow the directions. Use the definitions to help you.**

**Chord:** A line segment that passes through a circle and has endpoints on that circle

**Circumference:** The distance around a circle

**Diameter:** A chord that passes through the center of a circle

**Radius:** A line segment with one endpoint at the center of a circle and the other endpoint on the edge of the circle

6. Draw radius AB.

7. Draw diameter XY.

8. Trace the circumference.

9. Draw chord DE.

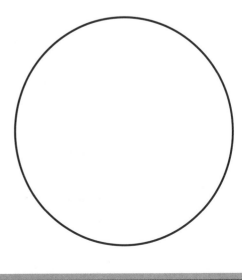

# DAY 14

**Write the name of an object that has each shape.**

10. cylinder _____

11. cube _____

12. cone _____

13. pyramid _____

14. rectangular prism _____

**Write the past tense of each irregular verb.**

15. write _____    16. teach _____

17. draw _____    18. find _____

19. speak _____    20. feel _____

21. hold _____    22. bend _____

23. hear _____    24. catch _____

**Write the past tense of each underlined verb.**

25. I <u>see</u> a butterfly on a flower.    _____

26. The butterfly <u>makes</u> her egg sticky.    _____

27. The tiny, white egg <u>sticks</u> to the leaf.    _____

**FITNESS FLASH:** Touch your toes 10 times.

* See page ii.

PLACE STICKER HERE

**Subtract to find each difference.**

| 1. | 4,314<br>− 2,532 | 2. | 3,826<br>− 49 | 3. | 2,182<br>− 396 | 4. | 5,433<br>− 25 |

| 5. | 6,922<br>− 5,833 | 6. | 22,318<br>− 17,725 | 7. | 57,260<br>− 23,458 | 8. | 68,011<br>− 14,343 |

**Write the singular possessive and the plural possessive of each noun.**

| | Singular | Possessive | | Plural | Possessive |
|---|---|---|---|---|---|
| **EXAMPLE:** | | | | | |
| | girl | *girl's* | | girls | *girls'* |
| 9. | key | | | keys | |
| 10. | bird | | | birds | |
| 11. | mouse | | | mice | |
| 12. | puppy | | | puppies | |
| 13. | woman | | | women | |
| 14. | class | | | classes | |

# DAY 15

Look at the picture clues. Write the singular form of each geometry term to complete the puzzle.

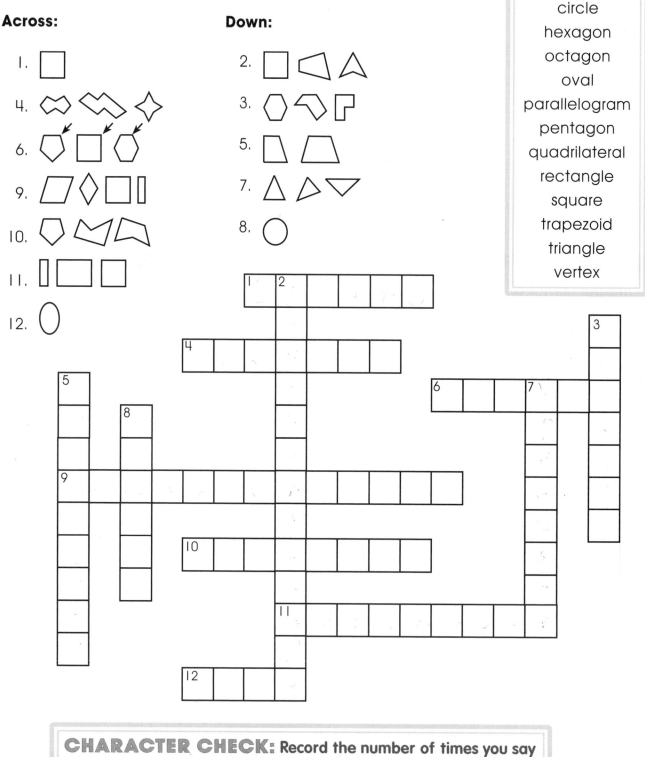

**Across:**

1.
4.
6.
9.
10.
11.
12.

**Down:**

2.
3.
5.
7.
8.

circle
hexagon
octagon
oval
parallelogram
pentagon
quadrilateral
rectangle
square
trapezoid
triangle
vertex

**CHARACTER CHECK:** Record the number of times you say "thank you" in one day. Share the results with a family member.

PLACE STICKER HERE

**Draw a line through the word that does not belong in each sentence.**

1.  All of the butterflies will be gone went by October.

2.  The state vegetable of Idaho is are the potato.

3.  She will hid hide behind the large, old tree.

4.  I have ridden rode my horse regularly this summer.

5.  Our dog constantly goes to that corner to dig digging.

**Read each pair of words. For each pair, write one way that the two things are alike and one way that they are different.**

6.  leopard and cheetah _____

_____

7.  keyboard and piano _____

_____

8.  cabin and tent _____

_____

9.  whistle and sing _____

_____

10. book and magazine _____

_____

# DAY 16

**Solve each problem.**

| 11. | 7,548 | 12. | 8,562 | 13. | 5,585 | 14. | 36,814 |
|---|---|---|---|---|---|---|---|
| | − 3,762 | | + 2,163 | | − 2,609 | | − 7,523 |

| 15. | 53,397 | 16. | 3,245 | 17. | 9,421 | 18. | 3,340 |
|---|---|---|---|---|---|---|---|
| | + 39,288 | | 5,029 | | 8,389 | | 7,189 |
| | | | + 6,981 | | + 4,506 | | + 4,482 |

---

**A past-tense verb expresses something that has already happened. Write the past or present tense of each verb.**

| Present | Past | | Present | Past |
|---|---|---|---|---|
| EXAMPLE: stay | *stayed* | 19. _____ | | thanked |
| 20. hop _____ | | 21. _____ | | called |
| 22. skate _____ | | 23. _____ | | sprained |
| 24. love _____ | | 25. _____ | | wrapped |
| 26. play _____ | | 27. _____ | | hugged |

**FACTOID:** Manhole covers are round so that they can't fall into the manholes.

PLACE STICKER HERE

**Replace each word in parentheses with a synonym.**

**EXAMPLE:** The man (said) _____ *yelled* _____ , "Watch out for that bee!"

1. Margaret (said) _____ , "Please come to my party."

2. Mother always (said) _____ , "A stitch in time saves nine."

3. "Is it already time to leave?" (said) _____ Casey.

4. "I don't like celery in soup," (said) _____ Dad.

5. "My kite is still in the air," (said) _____ Tony.

6. The boy with his mouth full of noodles (said) _____ that he wanted more.

**Every dictionary page has guide words at the top. They tell the first word on the page and the last word on the page. Write each word in alphabetical order under the correct guide words.**

| aggravate | aboard | about | aid | ailment |
|-----------|--------|-------|-----|---------|
| above | affect | after | agree | afford |

7. aardvark • afghan

8. Africa • aim

_____        _____

_____        _____

_____        _____

_____        _____

## DAY 17

**Read the passage. Then, answer the questions.**

### City Government

The president and the prime minister are important national leaders, but important leaders also live in your city. Many cities have mayors who are responsible for making decisions for the cities. They may also attend events such as parades or the openings of new libraries. A mayor often works with a group of people known as a city council. The members of the council are residents of different parts of the city who meet to plan activities and find solutions to any problems in the city. A city may also have a manager who makes sure that the city services are running smoothly. The city manager also creates a **budget** to plan how the city should spend its money. Other members of the city government include the chief of police and the fire chief. They make the rules that all police officers and firefighters must follow. A city needs many different people to work together to make life better for all of its citizens.

9. What is the main idea of this passage?

    a. The president is an important leader.

    b. The leader of the police is called a chief.

    c. City government includes many different people.

10. What does a mayor do? _____

11. Where do members of a city council come from?_____

12. What does a city manager do? _____

13. What is a budget?

    a. a plan that tells how a city should spend its money

    b. a parade

    c. the person who is the head of the fire department

**FITNESS FLASH:** Do arm circles for 30 seconds.

* See page ii.

PLACE STICKER HERE

**Multiply to find each product.**

1. $2 \times 4 \times 2 =$ _____
2. $3 \times 3 \times 5 =$ _____
3. $4 \times 2 \times 2 =$ _____
4. $2 \times 5 \times 1 =$ _____

5. $4 \times 2 \times 4 =$ _____
6. $2 \times 3 \times 7 =$ _____
7. $0 \times 9 \times 9 =$ _____
8. $3 \times 2 \times 3 =$ _____

9. $3 \times 3 \times 3 =$ _____
10. $5 \times 2 \times 2 =$ _____
11. $4 \times 2 \times 5 =$ _____
12. $2 \times 3 \times 6 =$ _____

13. $1 \times 2 \times 3 =$ _____
14. $3 \times 3 \times 0 =$ _____
15. $3 \times 5 \times 0 =$ _____
16. $1 \times 3 \times 5 =$ _____

17. $2 \times 3 \times 4 =$ _____
18. $2 \times 2 \times 3 =$ _____
19. $4 \times 3 \times 2 =$ _____
20. $8 \times 1 \times 8 =$ _____

**Write two sentences using the word *it's* and two sentences using the word *its*.**

**EXAMPLE:** *It's very hot outside today.*
*That shoe has lost its shoelaces.*

21. _____

22. _____

23. _____

24. _____

**Write two sentences using the word *eight* and two sentences using the word *ate*.**

25. _____

26. _____

27. _____

28. _____

# DAY 18

Write a story about taking a trip to outer space. Tell what kinds of things you should pack and how you should prepare. Describe where you would like to go and what you think it would be like there.

_____

_____

_____

_____

_____

_____

_____

_____

_____

_____

_____

_____

_____

_____

_____

**FACTOID:** You consume one-tenth of a calorie every time you lick a stamp.

PLACE
STICKER
HERE

**Read the passage. Then, answer the questions.**

### Nutrition

The food you eat helps your body grow. It gives you energy to work and play. Eating a variety of good foods each day will help you stay healthy. What you eat and how much food you need depend on whether you are a girl or a boy, how active you are, and your age. To find out what foods you should eat and how much food you need, go to *www.mypyramid.gov* and use the MyPyramid Plan calculator.

1. Why should you eat a variety of foods? _____

   _____

2. What are some things that can affect how much food you need? _____

   _____

3. From which food group did you eat the least today? _____

   _____

4. Which of your meals included the most food groups today? _____

   _____

**Circle each noun that should begin with a capital letter.**

5. My friends emmett and hugo want to join the boy scouts.

6. When his family was in idaho, rashad floated down snake river.

7. Does your cousin sierra go to winn elementary school?

8. Last night, doug stopped at brookstown mall to buy a gift.

9. I heard that ms. hernandez's class visited the lincoln memorial in washington, d.c.

10. Have you ever visited niagara falls in canada?

# DAY 19

**Solve each word problem.**

11. Jennifer bought a bag of apples for $2.50. The tax was 19¢. She used a coupon for 42¢ off. How much did she pay?

12. Bradley bought a shirt for $5 off the original price of $24. The tax was $1.40. How much did Bradley pay?

13. Elise has a job at the grocery store stocking shelves. She worked 4 hours on Wednesday and 5 hours on Friday. She earns $5 an hour. How much did she earn?

14. Gayle bought a six-pack of canned orange juice for $2.89. The store had a special for 74¢ off the original price. The tax was 60¢. How much did Gayle spend?

**Draw a line to connect each word to its meaning.**

**EXAMPLE:**

| | | |
|---|---|---|
| honorable | | a kind of lamp |
| 15. current | | to make clearly known |
| 16. knowledge | | having a good reputation |
| 17. suspicion | | occupation, source of livelihood |
| 18. exact | | leaving no room for error, accurate |
| 19. lantern | | now in progress |
| 20. profession | | information, awareness, understanding |
| 21. universal | | worldwide, understood by all |
| 22. agriculture | | the science and art of farming |
| 23. declare | | doubt |

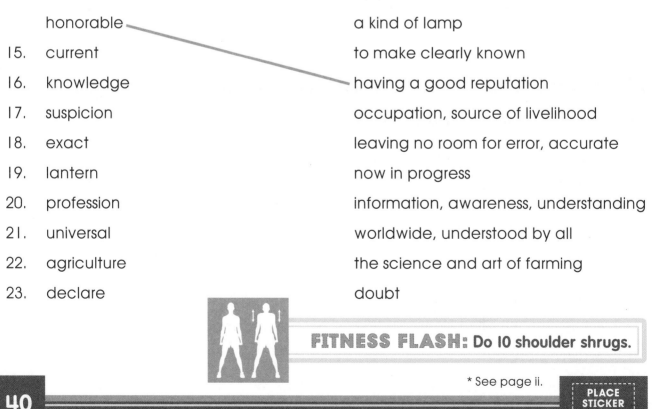

**FITNESS FLASH:** Do 10 shoulder shrugs.

* See page ii.

PLACE STICKER HERE

**Write the correct word for each definition.**

| admire | comfort | doubt | glisten | pedal | pause |

1. to have high regard for _____

2. a lever worked with the foot _____

3. shine or sparkle_____

4. to not believe; to feel uncertain_____

5. a short stop or wait _____

6. something that feels soft, like a cushion_____

The Continental Congress adopted the first official American flag on June 14, 1777. The American flag was a symbol of unity for the beginning nation.

**Design and draw your own flag. Then, write a paragraph on a separate sheet of paper explaining what your flag symbolizes. What do the colors mean? What do the images represent?**

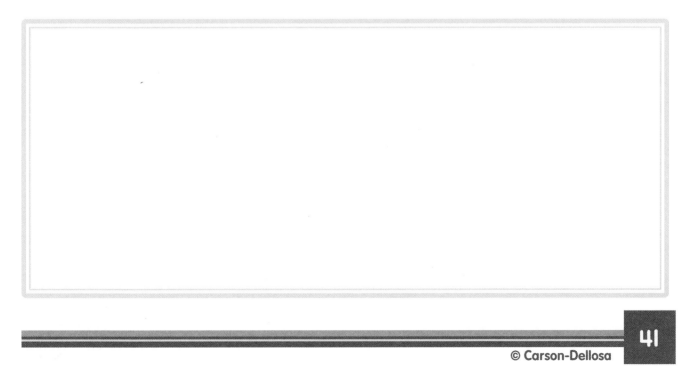

# DAY 20

**This Activity Pyramid works like the Food Pyramid. You can use the Activity Pyramid to help plan your summer exercise program. Fill in each blank.**

7. List one thing that is not good exercise that you could omit from your summer program.

a. _____

8. List three exercises that you could do to build strength and flexibility.

a. _____

b. _____

c. _____

9. List two sports in which you would like to participate.

a. _____

b. _____

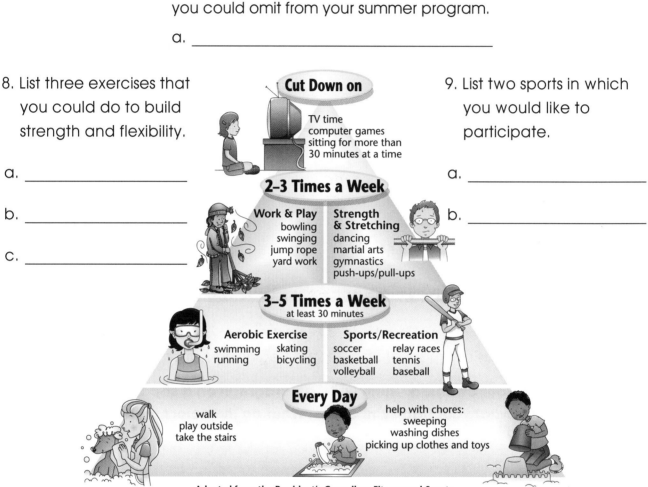

**Cut Down on**

TV time
computer games
sitting for more than
30 minutes at a time

**2–3 Times a Week**

**Work & Play**
bowling
swinging
jump rope
yard work

**Strength & Stretching**
dancing
martial arts
gymnastics
push-ups/pull-ups

**3–5 Times a Week**
at least 30 minutes

**Aerobic Exercise**
swimming    skating
running      bicycling

**Sports/Recreation**
soccer       relay races
basketball   tennis
volleyball   baseball

**Every Day**

walk
play outside
take the stairs

help with chores:
sweeping
washing dishes
picking up clothes and toys

Adapted from the President's Council on Fitness and Sports

List three everyday things that you could do to get moving more often.

10. _____

11. _____

12. _____

**CHARACTER CHECK:** Draw a picture of yourself with your best friend. Show your picture to an adult and explain why you like being friends with this person.

\* See page ii.

PLACE STICKER HERE

## Determining Your Heart Rate

Your heart is one of the most important organs in your body because it helps all of the other organs work. It is important to keep your heart pumping at a healthy rate. So, how do you know how fast your heart is pumping?

**Materials:**

- stopwatch or watch with a second hand

**Procedure:**

1. Place your index and middle fingers just under your jaw where it meets your neck. You should feel your heartbeat. A large artery that supplies blood to your brain is located there. Count the number of heart beats for six seconds. Multiply that number by 10 to determine your heart rate. Record your heart rate on the table below.

2. Now, measure how fast your heart beats after certain activities. Complete the table to track your results. Do each activity for one minute. Then, measure your heart rate using the six-second count.

| Activity | Number of beats in six seconds | Heartbeats per minute (multiply by 10) |
|---|---|---|
| Resting | | |
| Running in place | | |
| Jumping jacks | | |
| Push-ups | | |

**Conclusion:**

Your heart pumps blood, oxygen, and energy to your entire body. The more you exercise, the faster your heart needs to pump. That is why activities like running in place make your heart beat faster than it beats while resting. Running takes more energy than resting.

Continue this experiment with other activities. What increases your heart rate the most? The least? How do you feel when your heart is beating faster?

# BONUS

## Build a Backbone

Where would you be without a backbone? You would not be able to walk. You would not even be able to sit in a chair! The backbone is an amazing structure. Without it, you would not be able to do much of anything! Build a model backbone to see just how important it is.

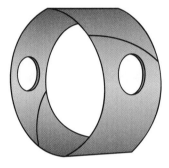

**Materials:**
- 11 cardboard tubes (short)
- Hole punch
- 11 rubber bands (2" or about 5 cm long)
- Scissors

**Procedure:**
1. Carefully cut each cardboard tube into thirds.
2. Punch two holes on opposite sides of each tube.
3. Loop the rubber bands together to form one long string. Thread the string of rubber bands through the holes in the tube sections, one at a time. When all of the sections are threaded on the rubber band string, tie off the string at the top and bottom.
4. Now, experiment with your model backbone. Bend it in different directions to see if it has any limitations. Try to figure out what would happen if one or more of the sections were damaged or had to be removed.

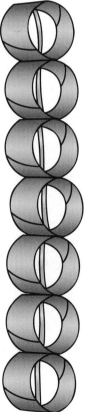

**Conclusion:**

The backbone serves as the major supporting structure in the body, which means it must possess a lot of rigidity. At the same time, it must be flexible to allow twisting, turning, and bending. The human spine has 33 vertebrae. They allow swaying and bending and, at the same time, provide support for the head and a place for the ribs and the pelvis to attach.

Research pictures of different animal vertebrae. How do your vertebrae compare to the vertebrae of a giraffe? How do they compare to the vertebrae of a snake?

## A Famous Place

**Research a famous world landmark. Take notes on the lines below. Then, design an advertisement that encourages travelers to visit that landmark. Include information about the landmark's location and interesting facts about its history.**

_____

_____

_____

# BONUS

## The Iditarod®

The Iditarod® is a dogsled race through Alaska. The chart below gives approximate distances between checkpoints along the race. Using the scale **I inch = 5 miles (8 km)**, determine how many lengths of the scale would be needed to show each distance on a map. Write your answers in the blanks below.

| Checkpoints | Distance between Checkpoints |
|---|---|
| Kaltag to Unalakleet | 90 miles (144.8 km) |
| Unalakleet to Shaktoolik | 40 miles (64.4 km) |
| Shaktoolik to Koyuk | 50 miles (80.5 km) |
| Koyuk to Elim | 50 miles (80.5 km) |
| Elim to Golovin | 30 miles (48.3 km) |
| Golovin to White Mountain | 20 miles (32.2 km) |
| White Mountain to Safety | 55 miles (88.5 km) |
| Safety to Nome | 20 miles (32.2 km) |

|  | | **Miles** | **Number of Lengths of I-inch scale** |
|---|---|---|---|
| I. | White Mountain to Safety | _____ | _____ |
| 2. | Koyuk to Elim | _____ | _____ |
| 3. | Safety to Nome | _____ | _____ |
| 4. | Unalakleet to Shaktoolik | _____ | _____ |
| 5. | Elim to Golovin | _____ | _____ |
| 6. | Golovin to White Mountain | _____ | _____ |
| 7. | Kaltag to Unalakleet | _____ | _____ |
| 8. | Shaktoolik to Koyuk | _____ | _____ |

# Time Zones

This map shows the time zones in the United States. Use this time zone map to answer each question.

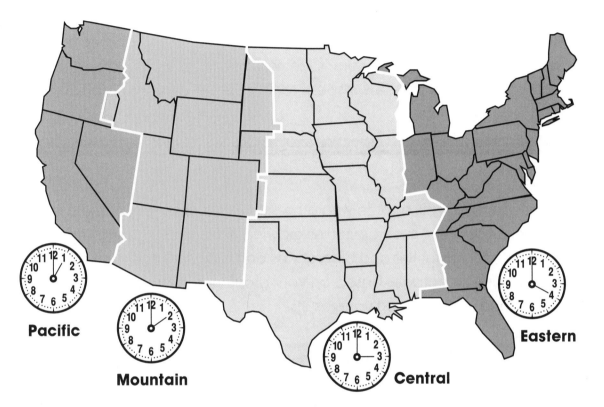

**Pacific** **Mountain** **Central** **Eastern**

1.  If it is 2:00 P.M. in Washington, D.C., what time is it in Alabama? _____

2.  If it is noon in California, what time is it in Wyoming? _____

3.  If it is 9:00 A.M. in Montana, what time is it in Iowa? _____

4.  If it is 6:00 P.M. in North Carolina, what time is it in Arizona? _____

5.  If it is 1:00 P.M. in Maine, what time is it in Nevada? _____

## BONUS

# Take It Outside!

By the time summer arrives, insects are very active. Take advantage of this time to observe a variety of insects. Fireflies, ants, and ladybugs and other beetles will provide you with many learning opportunities. Examine the insects and their habits. Look at what they eat and how they move. Make sure you do not touch or disturb the insects. Keep a journal to write your observations. Review what you have learned about different insects. You may find new respect for the largest class in the animal kingdom.

With an adult, go for a walk outside with a camera. Take a variety of pictures that make you think of summer, such as fireflies glowing in the late evening. After printing the pictures, look for similarities and differences and place the pictures into groups. Determine various percentages based on your groupings, such as what percent of the pictures contained water. Graph your results.

Summer is the perfect time of year to find a variety of healthful foods because many crops are harvested in the summer. With an adult, arrange to visit a local farmers' market, a plant nursery, or a garden supply store. Find out which foods grow best in your area. Talk to local farmers, gardeners, and grocers to learn about the importance of eating locally grown foods. Encourage your family to buy and eat those delicious, healthful foods.

* See page ii.

# Monthly Goals

Think of three goals to set for yourself this month. For example, you may want to exercise for 30 minutes each day. Write your goals on the lines and review them with an adult.

Place a sticker next to each goal that you complete. Feel proud that you have met your goals!

1. _____
PLACE STICKER HERE

2. _____
PLACE STICKER HERE

3. _____
PLACE STICKER HERE

# Word List

The following words are used in this section. They are good words for you to know. Read each word aloud. Use a dictionary to look up each word that you do not know. Then, write two sentences. Use a word from the word list in each sentence.

| | |
|---|---|
| community | material |
| descriptive | opinion |
| fraction | procedure |
| furrowed | transportation |

1. _____

_____

2. _____

_____

# Introduction to Strength

This section includes fitness and character development activities that focus on strength. These activities are designed to get you moving and thinking about strengthening your body and your character.

## Physical Strength

Like flexibility, strength is necessary for you to be healthy. You may think that a strong person is someone who can lift a lot of weight. However, strength is more than the ability to pick up heavy things. Strength is built over time. You are stronger now than you were in preschool. What are some activities that you can do now that you could not do then?

You can gain strength through everyday activities and many fun exercises. Carry grocery bags to build your arms. Ride a bike to strengthen your legs. Swim to strengthen your whole body. Exercises such as push-ups and chin-ups are also great strength builders.

Set goals this summer to improve your strength. Base your goals on activities you enjoy. Talk about your goals with an adult. As you meet your goals, set new ones. Celebrate your stronger, healthier body!

## Strength of Character

As you build your physical strength, work on your inner strength too. Having a strong character means standing up for who you are, even if others do not agree with your point of view.

You can show inner strength in many ways, such as being honest, supporting someone who needs your help, and putting your best efforts into every task. It is not always easy to show inner strength. Can you think of a time when you used inner strength to handle a situation, such as being teased by another child at the park?

Improve your inner strength over the summer. Think about ways you can show strength of character, such as having good sportsmanship in your baseball league. Reflect on your positive growth. Be proud of your strong character!

## Triceps Dip

Have an adult help you complete dips to strengthen your triceps, the muscles in the back of your arms. Find a sturdy chair or bench. If using a chair, have an adult hold the back of the chair for balance. Face away from the chair. Place both hands on the edge of the seat. Extend your legs so that you are holding yourself up with your arms. Lower your body until your upper arms are parallel to the seat. Then, push yourself up. Repeat several times to see how many dips you can complete. Try this activity several times each week. Keep track of your progress over the summer.

**A prefix is added to the beginning of a base word. A suffix is added to the end of a base word. Add the prefix *mis-*, *un-*, or *re-* to each word. Then, write a sentence using the whole word.**

1. _____lucky    _____

2. _____judge    _____

3. _____spell    _____

4. _____fill    _____

5. _____build    _____

**Add the suffix *-er*, *-less*, *-ful*, or *-ed* to each word. Then, write a sentence using the whole word.**

6. use _____    _____

7. spell _____    _____

* See page ii.

# DAY 1

An opinion is a belief or viewpoint that is not based on fact. You probably have many opinions about things, such as the best flavor of ice cream or which animal makes the best pet. People may be more willing to listen to and agree with your opinions if you state them clearly and persuasively. On a separate sheet of paper, write a three-paragraph persuasive essay on one of the topics provided.

1. People should always wear seat belts.
2. Children should be able to eat whatever they want.
3. Students should never have to do homework.
4. We should help people in other countries.

---

**FACTOID:** No word in the English language rhymes with *film, gulf,* or *wolf.*

PLACE STICKER HERE

**Multiply to find each product.**

| | | | | |
|---|---|---|---|---|
| 1.  12<br>    × 6 | 2.  12<br>    × 4 | 3.  22<br>    × 6 | 4.  18<br>    × 2 | 5.  23<br>    × 4 |
| 6.  23<br>    × 7 | 7.  34<br>    × 6 | 8.  16<br>    × 5 | 9.  78<br>    × 5 | 10.  86<br>    × 7 |
| 11.  69<br>    × 9 | 12.  57<br>    × 4 | 13.  62<br>    × 6 | 14.  97<br>    × 7 | 15.  83<br>    × 2 |

**The five senses are taste, touch, smell, sight, and hearing. Write a word from each of the five senses that describes each item.**

| EXAMPLE:<br>candy bar | taste<br>sweet | touch<br>smooth | smell<br>chocolate | sight<br>brown | sound<br>crunchy |
|---|---|---|---|---|---|

16.  a lemon _____

17.  an apple _____

18.  coffee _____

19.  bread _____

**Choose one item from the list and write a sentence about it. Be very descriptive and include the senses.**

_____

_____

# DAY 2

**Complete each table.**

20.  5 pennies = 1 nickel

| pennies | 5 | 10 | 15 | 20 | 25 | 30 |
|---------|---|----|----|----|----|----|
| nickels | 1 |    |    |    |    |    |

21.  10 dimes = 1 dollar

| dimes   | 10 | 20 | 30 |  |  |  |
|---------|----|----|----|--|--|--|
| dollars | 1  | 2  |    |  |  |  |

22.  6 cans of juice = 1 carton

| cans    | 6 | 12 |   | 24 |   | 36 |
|---------|---|----|---|----|---|----|
| cartons | 1 |    | 3 |    | 5 |    |

**When you write, it is important to express yourself clearly so that the reader can understand your meaning. Write a more descriptive word for each underlined word.**

**EXAMPLE:** This book is <u>good</u>.  *awesome*

23.  My teacher is <u>nice</u>.  _____

24.  Your <u>things</u> will be safe here.  _____

25.  This is a <u>big</u> building.  _____

26.  A car <u>went</u> by our house.  _____

27.  Our pictures of the trip turned out <u>badly</u>.  _____

**FITNESS FLASH:** Do 10 lunges.

\* See page ii.

PLACE STICKER HERE

**Use a metric ruler to measure each item.**

1. The length of your shoes _____

2. The length and width of this book _____ , _____

3. The width of your hand _____

4. Your kitchen table length and width _____ , _____

5. Your height in centimeters _____

**Find some other items to measure. First, try to guess each measurement and then use the ruler to see how close you were.**

| Item | Estimate | Measurement |
|------|----------|-------------|
| _____ | _____ | _____ |
| _____ | _____ | _____ |
| _____ | _____ | _____ |

**A pronoun takes the place of a noun. Underline each pronoun.**

6. Will you go with us?

7. A package came for us.

8. Tomorrow, we will go home.

9. We ate all of them.

10. He did a good job.

11. You are a good sport.

12. This book came for him.

13. It is time for her to go.

14. She went with me.

15. He and I ate the apples.

# DAY 3

**Most words have no meaning when they are spelled backward, but some words make new words. Write the pair of words for each clue.**

| bag | gab | loop | net | now | pat |
| pins | pool | snip | tap | ten | won |

**EXAMPLE:**

This word means *siesta*, but spelled backward, it means something that you cook in.

_____*nap*_____ & _____*pan*_____

16.  This word means something that you do to a dog, but spelled backward, it means something that you turn on to get water.

_____ & _____

17.  This word is a number, but spelled backward, it is something you use to catch a fish.

_____ & _____

18.  This word means *to chat*, but spelled backward, it is something that you use to carry things.

_____ & _____

19.  This word is a circle you make in shoelaces, but spelled backward, it is something that you swim in during the summer.

_____ & _____

20.  This word means *at once*, but spelled backward, it means *were victorious*.

_____ & _____

21.  This word is something you use for sewing, but spelled backward, it means *to cut*.

_____ & _____

**FACTOID:** Although a polar bear appears white, its skin is black, and its fur is actually made up of clear, hollow tubes.

PLACE STICKER HERE

**Personification is giving human characteristics to nonhuman things. Use personification to answer each question.**

1.  What would a pencil say to a hand? _____

    _____

2.  What would a carpet say to a foot? _____

    _____

3.  What would a basketball say to a basketball player? _____

    _____

4.  What would a skateboard say to a skateboarder? _____

    _____

**The earth already has many different kinds of insects, but there is always room for one more! Create a new insect. Write about what it looks like, where it lives, what it eats, and what predators it must avoid.**

_____

_____

_____

_____

_____

_____

_____

**DAY 4**

**Read the passage. Then, answer the questions.**

### Community Helpers

A community is a group of people who live in the same area or have the same interests. Communities need helpers to make everything function well. Some important community helpers are police officers and firefighters. Police officers make sure that everyone is following the laws of the community to keep people safe. Firefighters put out fires and educate people about fire safety. Other community helpers are people who work for the city, such as trash collectors and park rangers. Trash collectors drive down streets to collect everybody's trash. Park rangers make sure that city parks are clean and safe so that people can play or have picnics in them. Another important helper in the community is the librarian. The librarian makes sure that a lot of good books are available in the library for everyone in the community to read. The next time you see a community helper, say, "Thank you!"

5.  What is the main idea of this passage?

    a.  A community needs a lot of people to make it function well.

    b.  Police officers and firefighters are community helpers.

    c.  People like to have picnics in city parks.

6.  What is the role of police officers in a community? _____

    _____

7.  What is the role of firefighters in a community? _____

    _____

8.  How do trash collectors help the community? _____

    _____

9.  What do park rangers do for the community? _____

**FITNESS FLASH: Do 10 squats.**

* See page ii.

PLACE
STICKER
HERE

**Multiply to find each product.**

1.  4 × 10 = _____
2.  600 × 6 = _____
3.  7 × 800 = _____

4.  30 × 8 = _____
5.  5 × 20 = _____
6.  800 × 5 = _____

7.  8 × 90 = _____
8.  50 × 6 = _____
9.  600 × 5 = _____

10. 4 × 100 = _____
11. 7 × 80 = _____
12. 7 × 500 = _____

13. 900 × 7 = _____
14. 600 × 4 = _____
15. 900 × 4 = _____

16. 8 × 900 = _____
17. 800 × 2 = _____
18. 7 × 900 = _____

19. 3 × 10 = _____
20. 700 × 6 = _____
21. 3 × 800 = _____

22. 7 × 40 = _____
23. 9 × 10 = _____
24. 10 × 100 = _____

**The pronouns *I*, *you*, *he*, *she*, *it*, *we*, and *they* can be the subject of a sentence. Replace the underlined words in each sentence with a pronoun.**

25.  Antonio and I went fishing with our dad.

     _____

26.  The weather was sunny and warm.

     _____

27.  Connor and Miguel can help us with the bait.

     _____

28.  Mr. Simpson grew delicious tomatoes this year.

     _____

## DAY 5

**Look at the table about trees. Then, answer the questions.**

| Tree | Bark | Wood | Leaves |
|---|---|---|---|
| **Elm** | brown and rough | strong | oval shaped, saw-toothed edges, sharp points |
| **Birch** | creamy white, peels off in layers | elastic, won't break easily | heart shaped or triangular with pointed tips |
| **Oak** | dark gray, thick, rough, deeply furrowed | hard, fine grained | round, finger-shaped lobes |
| **Willow** | rough and broken | brown, soft, light | long, narrow, curved at tips |
| **Maple** | rough and gray | strong | in pairs, shaped like an open hand |
| **Hickory** | loose, peels off | white, hard | shaped like spearheads |
| **Holly** | ash colored | hard, fine grained | glossy, sharp tipped |

29.  Which tree has heart-shaped leaves? _____

30.  How many trees have hard wood? _____

31.  Which tree has sharp-tipped leaves? _____

32.  Which tree has wood like a rubber band? _____

33.  What are the different colors of bark? _____

34.  From which tree do you think we get syrup? _____

35.  Can you identify any of the trees from the table in your yard or your neighborhood? Which ones? _____

**CHARACTER CHECK:** Why do you think it is important to always be honest?

**Complete the multiplication table.**

| ✕ | 10 | 20 | 30 | 40 | 50 | 60 | 70 | 80 | 90 |
|---|----|----|----|----|----|----|----|----|----|
| 1 | 10 | 20 | | | | | 70 | | |
| 2 | | | | | | 120 | | | |
| 3 | | 60 | | | | | | | 270 |
| 4 | | | | 160 | | | | | |
| 5 | | | | | | 350 | | | |
| 6 | | | | | | | | | |
| 7 | | | 210 | | | | | | |
| 8 | | | | | 480 | | | | |
| 9 | | | 360 | | | | | | |

How does multiplying by hundreds differ from multiplying by tens? _____

_____

How could you change the table to show multiplying by hundreds? _____

_____

**Write *it's*, *its*, *your*, or *you're* to complete each sentence.**

1. I hope that _____ coming to my barn dance.

2. The dance will be for _____ friends also.

3. Do you think _____ too cold for a barn dance?

4. _____ starting time is 8 o'clock.

5. Will _____ family come to the dance with you?

6. _____ floor is long and wide.

# DAY 6

**Read the passage. Then, answer the questions.**

## World Holidays

The United States celebrates several special holidays every year. People in different countries, however, recognize different holidays. Many people in China celebrate a Lantern Festival to welcome the new year. Special lanterns are lit, and colorful parades march through the streets. In Scotland, some people celebrate Burns Night, which is a holiday in honor of the Scottish poet Robert Burns. Families or club members gather together for a special meal and a reading of Burns's poetry. Whereas the United States celebrates its independence on Independence Day (July 4), Canada celebrates Canada Day on July 1, the date that the government of Canada was created. On both Canada Day and Independence Day, people have community parades, picnics, and fireworks. People in some parts of Germany celebrate Oktoberfest to mark the harvest. They eat traditional German foods like sausages and potato salad. Immigrants brought their native foods and traditions when they left their homelands, so now many celebrate their old holidays in their new countries.

7. What is the main idea of this passage?

    a. Burns Night is a special holiday in Scotland.

    b. People around the world celebrate different holidays.

    c. Oktoberfest takes place in many cities.

8. What is a lantern?

    a. a type of food eaten in China

    b. a special holiday

    c. a type of lamp

9. How do people in Scotland honor Robert Burns? _____

    _____

    _____

**FACTOID:** Almonds are in the same family as peaches and roses.

PLACE STICKER HERE

**Write the abbreviation of each underlined word.**

Last <u>January</u> _____, we moved from <u>Georgia</u> _____ to

<u>New York</u> _____ . It was a very long trip. We left on <u>Monday</u> _____ ,

<u>March</u> _____ 30 and didn't get there until <u>Wednesday</u> _____ ,

<u>April</u> _____ 1.

On the trip, I had to learn how to measure. One day I measured

<u>gallons</u> _____ , <u>inches</u> _____ , <u>yards</u> _____ , and

<u>grams</u> _____ . I also learned about <u>adverbs</u> _____ and <u>adjectives</u>

_____ . It was a great trip!

We only drove about 20 <u>miles per hour</u> _____ . That is why it took us so long.

Also, we stopped at 1600 Pennsylvania <u>Avenue</u> _____ in Washington, <u>District</u>

<u>of Columbia</u> _____ . I think we should fly the next time!

**Use the table of contents to answer the questions.**

1. On what page would you find fast-food restaurants? _____

2. On what page could you find out what the weather is like? _____

3. On what page would you look for movie listings? _____

| Coraville Happenings Guide |
| --- |
| **Local Information, Table of Contents** |
| Entertainment ............................. 1 |
| Weather Conditions .................... 2 |
| Transportation ............................ 3 |
| Careers and Employment .......... 4 |
| Dining Out .................................. 5 |

4. On what page would you look for job openings? _____

5. On what page would you find bus schedules? _____

# DAY 7

An idiom is an expression that means something other than what the individual words literally say. Underline the idiom in each sentence. Then, write what the idiom means.

6. She was really pulling my leg.

   _____

7. Do you think we'll be in hot water?

   _____

8. Time flies when you are having fun.

   _____

9. You've hit the nail on the head, Shanice!

   _____

10. Ryan said that he will lend a hand tomorrow.

    _____

**Circle each sentence that is written in the future tense.**

11. Bob ran to the market.                Bob will run around the block.

12. I am having green beans for dinner.   I will have corn tomorrow.

13. Troy will catch the ball.             Troy catches the ball.

14. He may go to the new school.          He went to the new school.

15. Davion washed the dog.                Davion will wash the dog.

**FITNESS FLASH: Do five push-ups.**

\* See page ii.

PLACE STICKER HERE

**Write a word from the word bank to complete each sentence.**

| seconds | minutes | hours | days | weeks | months | years |

1. Phillip is in the fourth grade. He is 10 _____ old.

2. There are 30 _____ in June.

3. Nancy's baby brother started to walk at the age of 11 _____ .

4. There are 48 _____ in two days.

5. Nick's swimming lesson is 25 _____ long.

6. It took Leslie 10 _____ to comb her hair.

7. Every month has four _____ .

**Write each group of words in alphabetical order.**

8. events, evening, every, eventually

_____ _____ _____ _____

9. tremendous, treatment, tree, treasure

_____ _____ _____ _____

10. coast, coconut, coal, collect

_____ _____ _____ _____

11. entrance, entry, end, enthusiasm

_____ _____ _____ _____

## DAY 8

**Divide to find each quotient.**

12. 9 ÷ 3 = _____      90 ÷ 3 = _____      900 ÷ 3 = _____

13. 8 ÷ 2 = _____      80 ÷ 2 = _____      800 ÷ 2 = _____

14. 12 ÷ 4 = _____      120 ÷ 4 = _____      1,200 ÷ 4 =

15. 6 ÷ 3 = _____      60 ÷ 3 = _____      600 ÷ 3 = _____

16. 30 ÷ 6 = _____      300 ÷ 6 = _____      3,000 ÷ 6 = _____

17. 72 ÷ 8 = _____      720 ÷ 8 = _____      7,200 ÷ 8 = _____

18. 32 ÷ 8 = _____      320 ÷ 8 = _____      3,200 ÷ 8 = _____

19. 49 ÷ 7 = _____      490 ÷ 7 = _____      4,900 ÷ 7 = _____

**Look up the word *meet* in a dictionary. After each sentence, write whether *meet* is a noun or a verb.**

**EXAMPLE:** I will meet you at three.     *verb*

20. Tomorrow, we are going to have a track meet.     _____

21. I hope he meets his group on time.     _____

22. We have a swim meet at 7:00 P.M.     _____

23. He will have to meet the payments every month.     _____

24. It was nice to meet and talk with you yesterday.     _____

25. Are you going to meet your friends later?     _____

**FACTOID:** Millions of trees are accidentally planted by squirrels because they forget where they hid the nuts!

PLACE STICKER HERE

**Divide to find each quotient.**

EXAMPLE:
```
   12 R 2
3)38
  -3
   8
  -6
   2
```

1. 3)95

2. 4)47

3. 4)85

4. 5)58

5. 2)65

6. 9)100

7. 7)79

8. 5)57

**Write each word on the line. Draw a line between each syllable in the word. Use a dictionary to check your work.**

EXAMPLE: column _____col/umn_____

9. harness _____

10. liveliness _____

11. inflate _____

12. cable _____

13. glorious _____

14. washing _____

15. pigeon _____

16. apple _____

17. jewelry _____

18. maple _____

19. bicycle _____

20. frozen _____

21. difficult _____

22. tennis _____

23. happy _____

Look up the word *power* in a dictionary. Now, write a paragraph about someone or something that has power. Explain why you think this person or thing has power and how you think that came to be.

_____

_____

_____

_____

_____

_____

_____

_____

_____

_____

_____

_____

_____

**FITNESS FLASH:** Do 10 sit-ups.

* See page ii.

PLACE STICKER HERE

The next time you watch TV or read a magazine, pay attention to the commercials or advertisements. In each box, write what you think is true and what you think is false about each commercial or advertisement you watched.

| What is the commercial or advertisement about? | True | False |
|---|---|---|
| 1. | | |
| 2. | | |
| 3. | | |

Write three ways to conserve each resource.

4. water _____

_____

5. trees _____

_____

6. oil _____

_____

7. wildlife habitats _____

_____

# DAY 10

**Read the passage. Then, answer the questions.**

## Planning a City

What do the streets in your city or town look like? Some cities have streets that are very straight and organized. It is easy to get from one point to another. Other cities have streets that seem to go nowhere. Usually when streets are planned in a city or town, a grid system is used. One example of a grid system can be found in Philadelphia, Pennsylvania, which is divided into four sections around a central square. William Penn created the design in 1682. Penn's grid included wide streets that were easy for people to walk on. Penn was originally from London, England, and he considered its confusing maze of narrow streets too difficult to navigate. Penn wanted to make sure that people could get around the city easily and safely. Many other cities used Penn's grid when they designed their street systems.

8. What is the main idea of this passage?

   a. William Penn drew the first grid system.

   b. Some cities use grid systems to organize their streets.

   c. Some streets are straight and organized.

9. What is one good thing about having wide streets? _____

   _____

10. What is a grid system?

    a. a way of arranging straight streets in a town or city

    b. a maze of narrow streets

    c. a famous street in London

11. What did Penn not like about the streets in London?_____

    _____

**CHARACTER CHECK:** Why is it important to be someone whom people can trust? How can you get and maintain a positive reputation? Write your answers on a separate sheet of paper.

**Write the fraction that describes each shaded section.**

**EXAMPLE:**

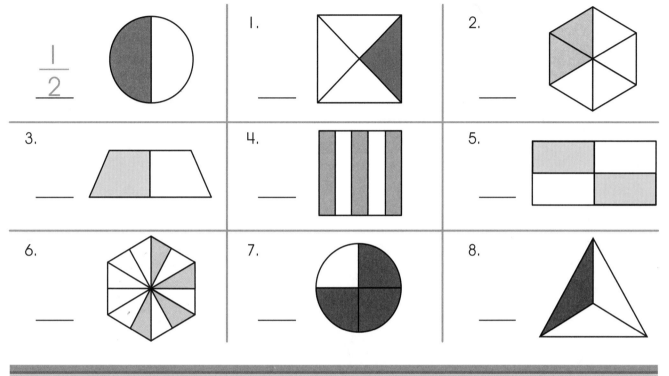

$\dfrac{1}{2}$

1. ___

2. ___

3. ___

4. ___

5. ___

6. ___

7. ___

8. ___

**Read each clue and write the mystery word.**

- It is composed of mineral particles that are mixed with animal and plant matter.

- It is a well-organized, complicated layer of debris that covers most of the earth's land surface.

- It can be red or black, as well as many other shades and colors.

- It is one of the most important resources in any country.

- It takes a long time to form.

- Geologists say that it is the material that covers the rock below the earth's surface.

9. Answer: _____

## DAY 11

**Label each angle.**

**Right Angle:** Angle that measures 90 degrees (the angle forms a square corner)

**Acute Angle:** Angle that measures less than a right angle, or less than 90 degrees

**Obtuse Angle:** Angle that measures more than 90 degrees but less than 180 degrees, or greater than a right angle

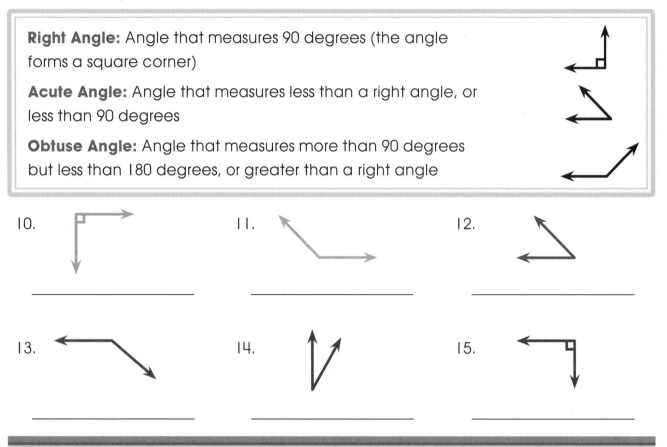

10. _____

11. _____

12. _____

13. _____

14. _____

15. _____

**The air contains water. Try this experiment to discover how water gets into the air.**

• Get three or more drinking glasses that are all about the same size.

• Fill the glasses almost full of water.

• Place them in different areas, such as warm places, cool places, dark places, windy places, outside places, inside places, and other places of your choice.

• Watch them for four or five days. Check the water levels.

**What happened to the water in the glasses? On a separate sheet of paper, explain in your own words where you think the water vapor in the atmosphere comes from and where it goes.**

**FACTOID:** Adults blink about 10 times a minute, but babies blink only once or twice a minute.

PLACE STICKER HERE

**Write >, <, or = to compare each pair of fractions. Use the fraction table for help.**

1.  $\frac{1}{2} \bigcirc \frac{1}{4}$    2.  $\frac{2}{3} \bigcirc \frac{1}{3}$

3.  $\frac{1}{4} \bigcirc \frac{1}{6}$    4.  $\frac{2}{6} \bigcirc \frac{1}{3}$

5.  $\frac{4}{8} \bigcirc \frac{2}{10}$    6.  $\frac{1}{12} \bigcirc \frac{1}{10}$

7.  $\frac{3}{4} \bigcirc \frac{2}{8}$    8.  $\frac{2}{5} \bigcirc \frac{1}{3}$

9.  $\frac{3}{8} \bigcirc \frac{10}{12}$    10.  $\frac{2}{8} \bigcirc \frac{1}{4}$

11.  $\frac{1}{5} \bigcirc \frac{2}{10}$    12.  $\frac{1}{3} \bigcirc \frac{2}{4}$

| $\frac{1}{2}$ | | | | | $\frac{1}{2}$ | | | |
| $\frac{1}{3}$ | | | $\frac{1}{3}$ | | | $\frac{1}{3}$ | | |
| $\frac{1}{4}$ | | $\frac{1}{4}$ | | $\frac{1}{4}$ | | $\frac{1}{4}$ | | |
| $\frac{1}{5}$ | $\frac{1}{5}$ | | $\frac{1}{5}$ | | $\frac{1}{5}$ | | $\frac{1}{5}$ | |
| $\frac{1}{6}$ | $\frac{1}{6}$ | $\frac{1}{6}$ | $\frac{1}{6}$ | $\frac{1}{6}$ | $\frac{1}{6}$ | | | |
| $\frac{1}{8}$ | $\frac{1}{8}$ | $\frac{1}{8}$ | $\frac{1}{8}$ | $\frac{1}{8}$ | $\frac{1}{8}$ | $\frac{1}{8}$ | $\frac{1}{8}$ | |
| $\frac{1}{10}$ | $\frac{1}{10}$ | $\frac{1}{10}$ | $\frac{1}{10}$ | $\frac{1}{10}$ | $\frac{1}{10}$ | $\frac{1}{10}$ | $\frac{1}{10}$ | $\frac{1}{10}$ $\frac{1}{10}$ |
| $\frac{1}{12}$ | $\frac{1}{12}$ | $\frac{1}{12}$ | $\frac{1}{12}$ | $\frac{1}{12}$ | $\frac{1}{12}$ | $\frac{1}{12}$ | $\frac{1}{12}$ | $\frac{1}{12}$ $\frac{1}{12}$ $\frac{1}{12}$ $\frac{1}{12}$ |

**Words in a series are separated by commas. Write the commas in each sentence.**

13.  Lin Paco Julie and Keesha are going to a movie.

14.  Anna took her spelling reading and math books to school.

15.  The snack bar is only open Monday Tuesday Friday and Saturday.

16.  Our new school flag is blue green yellow black and orange.

17.  Many women men children and pets enjoy sledding.

18.  Have you seen the kittens chicks or goslings?

**Read the passage. Then, answer the questions.**

### Bird Watching

Many people enjoy the hobby of bird watching. It is a pastime you can do in your own yard. If you put seeds in a bird feeder or hang a birdhouse, you are more likely to attract birds. You may notice that birds visit the feeder at certain times of day or that different birds prefer different types of foods. You may see baby birds trying their wings as they leave the nest for the first time. Some people travel to other parts of the world to see birds that they cannot see at home. They may use binoculars to get a better look at birds perching in trees or flying overhead. Some people keep lists of the species of birds they have seen. There are even contests to see who can spot the most different birds over a period of time!

19.  What is the main idea of this passage?

    a.  Bird watching is a popular hobby that many people enjoy.

    b.  Some birds like to eat seeds, while others like fruit.

    c.  There are many different species of birds.

20.  How can you attract more birds to your yard? _____

_____

21.  What are some things you might notice about birds in your yard?

_____

_____

22.  What do people use to help them see birds from a distance? _____

**FITNESS FLASH:** Do 10 lunges.

* See page ii.

PLACE STICKER HERE

**Multiply to find each product.**

| 1. | 162<br>× 5 | 2. | 398<br>× 2 | 3. | 904<br>× 8 | 4. | 329<br>× 5 |
|---|---|---|---|---|---|---|---|

| 5. | 240<br>× 7 | 6. | 432<br>× 6 | 7. | 412<br>× 8 | 8. | 542<br>× 9 |
|---|---|---|---|---|---|---|---|

**When you categorize words, you put them in groups under a common heading.**
**Categorize these words under each heading.**

| interstate | speed | equal to | insect | candidate |
|---|---|---|---|---|
| debate | estimate | hexagon | basin | highway |
| environment | freedom | society | elevation | equator |
| measure | region | colony | bacteria | yield |
| numerator | hemisphere | larva | recycle | intersection |

| Math | Geography | Transportation | Science | Social Studies |
|---|---|---|---|---|
| _____ | _____ | _____ | _____ | _____ |
| _____ | _____ | _____ | _____ | _____ |
| _____ | _____ | _____ | _____ | _____ |
| _____ | _____ | _____ | _____ | _____ |
| _____ | _____ | _____ | _____ | _____ |

# DAY 13

**The letters in each of these words are in alphabetical order. Unscramble the letters to write each word correctly. The first letter of the word is underlined.**

| | | | | |
|---|---|---|---|---|
| represent | remember | factory | serious | difficult |
| whistle | magazine | unbroken | industry | thought |

**EXAMPLE:**

abbelop*r*     *probable*

9. aaegi<u>m</u>nz _____

10. eior<u>s</u>su _____

11. eeenp<u>r</u>rst _____

12. ghho<u>t</u>tu _____

13. beeemm<u>r</u>r _____

14. beknnor<u>u</u> _____

15. ac<u>f</u>orty _____

16. c<u>d</u>ffiilut _____

17. d<u>i</u>nrstuy _____

18. ehilst<u>w</u> _____

## Fact vs. Fiction

Honesty means telling the truth. Imagine that you and a friend are at the movies. Each of you orders a bag of popcorn, and the cashier accidentally gives you extra change. What do you do?

On another sheet of paper, draw two comic strips that start the same but end differently. The first comic should show the outcome of not being honest, and the second should show the outcome of being honest. Include at least four scenes in each comic strip to capture your thoughts.

**FACTOID:** The world's largest desert is the Sahara. It covers 3.5 million square miles (9 million km²) or about one-third of Africa.

PLACE STICKER HERE

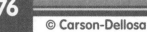

Use a stopwatch or a watch with a second hand to time yourself as you do the following activities. Use that information to calculate how many times you could do them in 5 minutes, 8 minutes, 10 minutes, and 15 minutes.

1. How many times can you hop in one minute? _____

2. How many steps can you take in one minute? _____

3. How many jumping jacks can you do in one minute? _____

4. How many times can you toss a ball and catch it in one minute? _____

5. How many times can you bounce a ball in one minute? _____

| Activity | Minutes | | | | |
|---|---|---|---|---|---|
| | 1 | 5 | 8 | 10 | 15 |
| hop | | | | | |
| steps (walking) | | | | | |
| jumping jacks | | | | | |
| toss and catch ball | | | | | |
| bounce ball | | | | | |

A comma belongs after the words *yes* and *no* when they begin a sentence. A comma also belongs before and/or after a person's name when the person is being addressed. Write commas where they belong in each sentence.

6. Yes I will go with you Tristan.

7. Wynona I am glad that Zoe is here.

8. Aaron do you play tennis?

9. Yes I went to the doctor's office.

10. Raul do you want to go?

11. Neyla what happened?

12. No I never learned how to fish.

13. Mom thanks for the help.

14. No I need to finish this.

15. Hugo I found a penny.

16. Come on T.J. let's go to the game.

17. Tell me Crystal did you do this?

## DAY 14

Write a story about your family. Tell who your family members are and what they are like.

_____

_____

_____

_____

_____

_____

_____

_____

_____

_____

_____

_____

**FITNESS FLASH:** Do 10 squats.

* See page ii.

PLACE
STICKER
HERE

**Follow the directions to draw a new figure.**

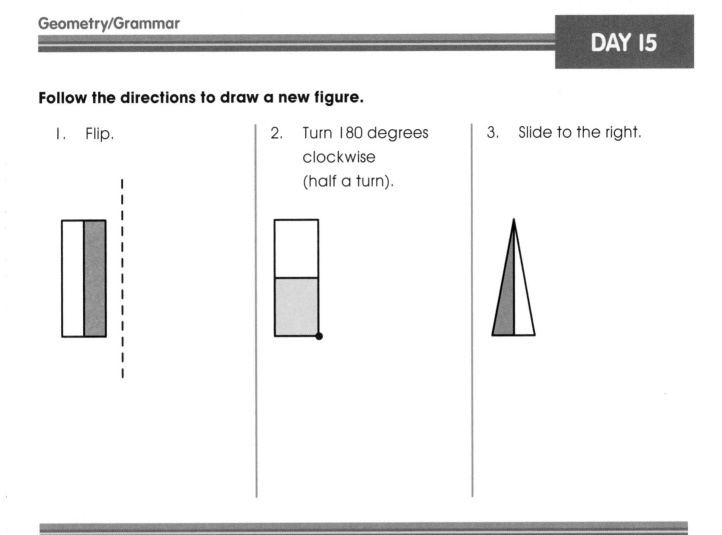

1. Flip.

2. Turn 180 degrees clockwise (half a turn).

3. Slide to the right.

**Write any missing periods, question marks, exclamation points, commas, quotation marks, or capitalization in each sentence.**

4. Nate, do you have the map of our town asked Kit

5. What an exciting day I had cried Janelle

6. I said the puppy chewed up my sneaker

7. Did you know that birds' bones are hollow asked Mrs. Tyler

8. She answered no I did not know that

9. Wayne exclaimed I won first prize in the pie-baking contest

10. I'm tired after raking the yard said Sadie

11. I am too replied Sarah

**Read the passage. Then, answer the questions.**

### Science Experiments

Scientists learn about the world by conducting experiments. They take careful notes about the instruments they use and the results they find. They share their discoveries with others so that everyone learns more about their subjects. You can do experiments too! The library has many books with safe experiments that use balloons, water, or baking soda. You can learn how light travels or why marbles roll down a ramp. Ask an adult to help you choose and set up an experiment and to watch to make sure you are being safe. Be sure to clean up the area and wash your hands afterward. Take good notes about your work. By changing only one thing, the next time you do the experiment, you may get a completely different result. The important thing is not to worry if your results are not what you expected. Some of the greatest scientific discoveries in the world were made by accident!

12. What is the main idea of this passage?

   a. Children can do experiments as long as they are safe.

   b. Scientists often make mistakes that lead to great discoveries.

   c. You should always take good notes when conducting an experiment.

13. What kinds of information do scientists write in their notes? _____

_____

14. What happens when scientists share their findings with others? _____

_____

15. Why should you ask an adult to help? _____

_____

**CHARACTER CHECK:** At the beginning of one day, tell a family member three good things that are going to happen to you that day.

PLACE STICKER HERE

**Write the month or the name of each U.S. holiday or special day. Use a calendar if you need help.**

1. Be sure to wear green on March 17. It's_____ .

2. Send your sweetheart a card on February 14. It's_____ .

3. On July 4, the United States celebrates _____ .

4. October 31 can be really scary. It's _____ .

5. Do you work on _____ in September?

6. Martin Luther King Jr.'s birthday is in_____ .

7. Americans celebrate this parent's day in June. _____

**Circle the word that is on the dictionary page with each pair of guide words.**

8. bowling • brain

   bread        braid        brave

9. liquid • litter

   list        live        lion

10. monster • more

    money     monsoon     moon

11. work • worst

    word        world        worth

12. gold • gossamer

    gondola     goal     gourd

13. spoon • spread

    spoil        spring        spray

14. flank • flaw

    flash        flame        flight

15. central • chafe

    cell        chalet        certain

# DAY 16

**Circle the two words in each group that are spelled correctly.**

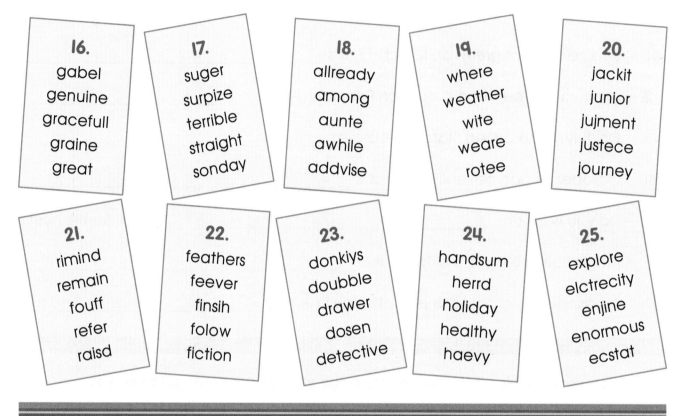

**16.**
gabel
genuine
gracefull
graine
great

**17.**
suger
surpize
terrible
straight
sonday

**18.**
allready
among
aunte
awhile
addvise

**19.**
where
weather
wite
weare
rotee

**20.**
jackit
junior
jujment
justece
journey

**21.**
rimind
remain
fouff
refer
raisd

**22.**
feathers
feever
finsih
folow
fiction

**23.**
donkiys
doubble
drawer
dosen
detective

**24.**
handsum
herrd
holiday
healthy
haevy

**25.**
explore
elctrecity
enjine
enormous
ecstat

**Circle the pronoun that correctly completes each sentence.**

26.   Lily and (I, me) like to visit museums.

27.   (They, Them) were very juicy oranges.

28.   He helped her and (I, me).

29.   (We, Us) tried not to fall as much this time.

30.   Miss Green gave a shovel and a bucket to (he, him).

31.   (I, Me) wanted a horse for my birthday.

32.   Rick asked (she, her) to come with us.

**FACTOID:** Hummingbirds are the only birds that can hover and fly upside down.

PLACE
STICKER
HERE

**Write each missing numerator.**

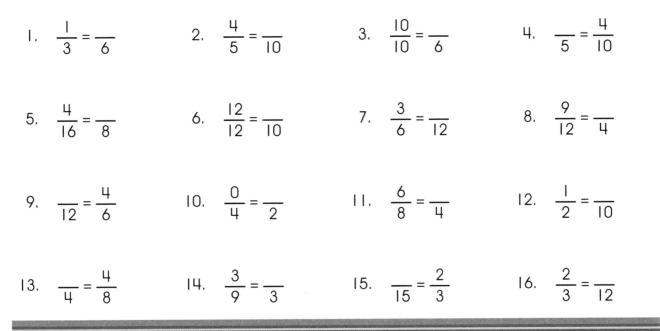

1.  $\dfrac{1}{3} = \dfrac{}{6}$

2.  $\dfrac{4}{5} = \dfrac{}{10}$

3.  $\dfrac{10}{10} = \dfrac{}{6}$

4.  $\dfrac{}{5} = \dfrac{4}{10}$

5.  $\dfrac{4}{16} = \dfrac{}{8}$

6.  $\dfrac{12}{12} = \dfrac{}{10}$

7.  $\dfrac{3}{6} = \dfrac{}{12}$

8.  $\dfrac{9}{12} = \dfrac{}{4}$

9.  $\dfrac{}{12} = \dfrac{4}{6}$

10.  $\dfrac{0}{4} = \dfrac{}{2}$

11.  $\dfrac{6}{8} = \dfrac{}{4}$

12.  $\dfrac{1}{2} = \dfrac{}{10}$

13.  $\dfrac{}{4} = \dfrac{4}{8}$

14.  $\dfrac{3}{9} = \dfrac{}{3}$

15.  $\dfrac{}{15} = \dfrac{2}{3}$

16.  $\dfrac{2}{3} = \dfrac{}{12}$

**Write the correct word for each definition.**

| schedule | campaign | artificial | reputation |
|---|---|---|---|
| assistant | exchange | publicize | genuine |

17.  not natural, not real _____

18.  a timed plan for a project _____

19.  a giving or taking of one thing for another _____

20.  an opinion in which a person is commonly held _____

21.  a person who serves or helps _____

22.  being what it is said to be; true or real _____

23.  a series of planned actions, often to get someone elected _____

24.  to make information known _____

**Read the passage. Then, answer the questions.**

### Eclipses

An eclipse happens when Earth and the moon line up with the sun. A lunar eclipse occurs when Earth moves between the sun and the moon. Earth blocks some sunlight from reaching the moon, so the moon appears dark from Earth's shadow. A solar eclipse occurs when the moon moves between Earth and the sun. The moon blocks some sunlight from reaching Earth, so the sky grows dark. It is safe to view a lunar eclipse, but you should never look directly at a solar eclipse, even through sunglasses. Instead, make a pinhole projector. Cut a small square in the middle of a piece of cardboard. Place a piece of aluminum foil across the square, and then poke a small hole in the foil. Let the sun's light shine through the hole onto another piece of cardboard. You can safely look at the sun's image on the second piece of cardboard.

25. What is the main idea of this passage?

    a. You should never look directly at the sun.

    b. An eclipse happens when sunlight is blocked by Earth or the moon.

    c. The sky grows dark during a solar eclipse.

26. When does a lunar eclipse occur? _____

    _____

27. What does the moon look like during a lunar eclipse? _____

    _____

28. When does a solar eclipse occur? _____

    _____

**FITNESS FLASH:** Do five push-ups.

* See page ii.

PLACE STICKER HERE

**Closed figures that have straight lines are called polygons. Circle the polygons.**

a.    b.    c.    d.    e.

1.  Why are they polygons? _____

**A vertex is where each side of a polygon meets. Count and write the number of sides and the number of vertices in each polygon.**

| triangle | pentagon | quadrilateral | octagon |
|----------|----------|---------------|---------|

2.  sides _____          3.  sides _____          4.  sides _____          5.  sides _____

vertices _____          vertices _____          vertices _____          vertices _____

**Book titles should be underlined, and all important words and verbs in titles should be capitalized. The first and last words of a title are always capitalized too. Rewrite each title correctly.**

6.  millions of cats _____

7.  higher than the arrow _____

8.  john paul jones _____

9.  no flying in the house _____

10.  ludo and the star horse _____

11.  an elephant is not a cat _____

12.  one wide river to cross _____

13.  the tropic express _____

# DAY 18

A simile is a figure of speech that compares two things using the words *as* or *like*. Complete each simile.

**EXAMPLE: The bedsheets were as white as a snowy owl.**

14. Her eyes were like _____

15. The night was as dark as _____

16. His legs were as _____

---

**It is a good idea to have a first-aid kit in your home. A first-aid kit contains supplies, such as bandages and ointments, that would help you in an emergency. Make a list of the things you would put in your first-aid kit and explain why.**

_____

_____

_____

_____

_____

_____

_____

_____

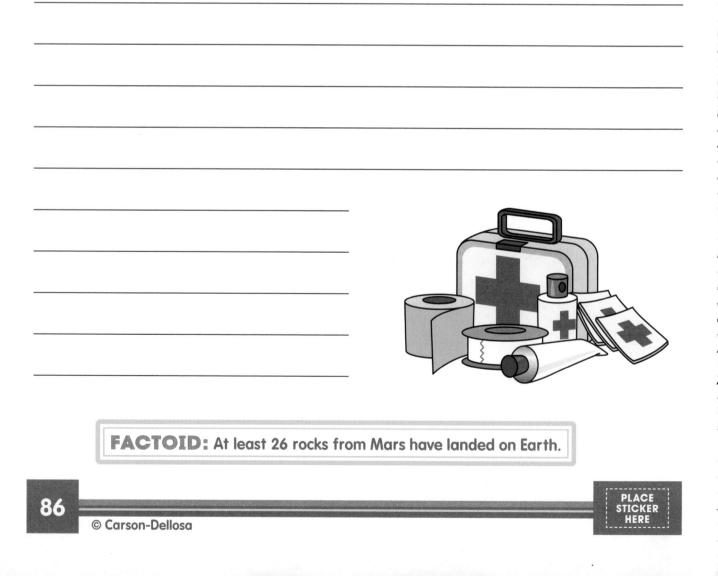

**FACTOID: At least 26 rocks from Mars have landed on Earth.**

PLACE STICKER HERE

**Circle each abbreviation.**

1. Dr. Fox is my family doctor.

2. Do you live on Rocksberry Rd.?

3. My teacher's name is Ms. Hansen.

4. On Mon., we are taking a trip to Fort Worth, TX.

5. Will Mr. Harris sell his company to your parents?

**Write the abbreviation for each word.**

6. Avenue _____   7. tablespoon _____

8. Tuesday _____   9. January _____

10. Mister _____   11. Street _____

12. teaspoon _____   13. Thursday _____

**Chart the outside temperature for four weeks. Use the Internet or the news for the temperatures each day. Write the high and low temperatures in the table.**

| Sun. | Mon. | Tues. | Wed. | Thurs. | Fri. | Sat. |
|------|------|-------|------|--------|------|------|
|      |      |       |      |        |      |      |
|      |      |       |      |        |      |      |
|      |      |       |      |        |      |      |
|      |      |       |      |        |      |      |

# DAY 19

A survey is a series of questions about a product or an issue. Conduct a survey of your neighbors, friends, or relatives on how many pets they have and what kind. Think of questions you can ask. Use the space below to take notes. Then, record the results in a report, chart, graph, table, or picture.

**FITNESS FLASH:** Do 10 sit-ups.

\* See page ii.

PLACE STICKER HERE

**Convert each improper fraction to a mixed number.**

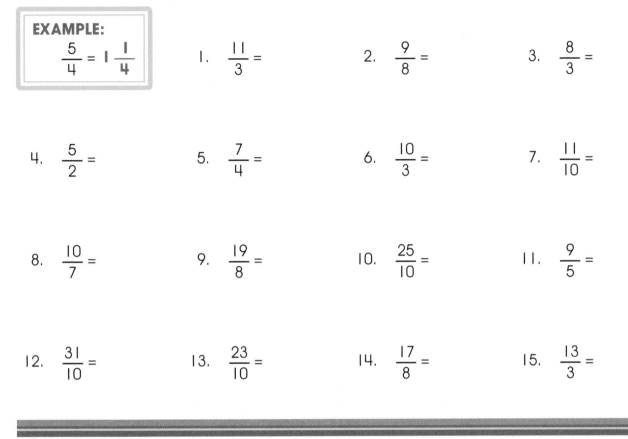

EXAMPLE:
$$\frac{5}{4} = 1\frac{1}{4}$$

1. $\frac{11}{3} =$

2. $\frac{9}{8} =$

3. $\frac{8}{3} =$

4. $\frac{5}{2} =$

5. $\frac{7}{4} =$

6. $\frac{10}{3} =$

7. $\frac{11}{10} =$

8. $\frac{10}{7} =$

9. $\frac{19}{8} =$

10. $\frac{25}{10} =$

11. $\frac{9}{5} =$

12. $\frac{31}{10} =$

13. $\frac{23}{10} =$

14. $\frac{17}{8} =$

15. $\frac{13}{3} =$

## Worth the "Weight"

Try adding a strength component to any physical activity. The next time you are ready to play or exercise, put on a backpack filled with soft, slightly weighted objects, such as small bags of sand. You will notice a small difference while you play or exercise. But, by the end of the summer, you will notice a big difference in your strength, especially if you gradually add more weight each time you exert yourself.

* See page ii.

## DAY 20

**Complete each sentence by circling the word that is spelled correctly.**

16. The big cat couldn't _____ the tree.

    a. climb      b. climbe      c. climmb      d. clibm

17. We paid $100 for _____ .

    a. groseries    b. groceeries   c. groceries    d. grosserys

18. Chad is a very _____ person.

    a. kreative      b. creative      c. createive      d. crative

19. We love to _____ ride in the winter.

    a. sleigh      b. sleia      c. cleigh      d. slagh

20. I found the perfect _____ for my science project.

    a. matterial    b. maririal    c. metariel    d. material

**Make a list of things that use electricity. Then, write about what you think life would be like without electricity.**

_____

_____

_____

_____

_____

**CHARACTER CHECK:** What does it mean to be a good friend? On a separate sheet of paper, make a list of 10 traits that a good friend should have. Why are these traits important for a strong friendship?

PLACE STICKER HERE

## Trust Metal to Rust

**Will iron nails placed in water rust faster and lose more mass than iron nails placed in sand?**

### Materials:

- 2 identical glass jars
- 10 iron nails
- 200 mL (6.75 ounces) of distilled water
- balance
- paper towels
- 200 mL (6.75 ounces) of very dry sand

### Procedure:

1. Put 200 mL of sand into one jar and 200 mL of water into the other jar.

2. Use the balance to find the mass of five nails. Record the mass in the table. Place the nails in the sand in the first jar.

3. Use the balance to find the mass of the remaining five nails. Record the mass in the table. Place the second group of nails in the water in the second jar. Leave both jars in a safe place overnight.

4. The next day, remove the nails from the jar of sand. Place them on a clean, dry paper towel. Remove excess sand but do not rub the nails.

5. Place the nails on the balance. Record their mass on the data table. Then, place the nails back into the jar of sand. Repeat with the nails in the jar of water.

6. Continue to collect data for three more days. Record your results in the table.

| Day | Nails in Sand | | Nails in Water | |
|---|---|---|---|---|
| | Mass | Observations | Mass | Observations |
| 1 | | | | |
| 2 | | | | |
| 3 | | | | |
| 4 | | | | |
| 5 | | | | |

## BONUS

### Screening the Sun

There are many different brands of sunscreen with various SPF ratings. The SPF, or sun protection factor, tells you how long the sunscreen will protect your skin. To find out if higher SPF sunscreens really provide better protection, try the following experiment.

**Materials:**
- 4 ultraviolet (UV) detection beads (available from scientific supply companies)
- 3 bottles of sunscreen (the same brand with different SPFs)
- tray (lined with paper)
- stopwatch

**Procedure:**
1. Obtain four UV beads of the same color. These beads are coated with a special chemical that makes them change color when exposed to UV light. The darker the color, the stronger the UV light.
2. Rub a small amount of one sunscreen over a bead and place it on the lined tray. Label the bead with the sunscreen's SPF. Repeat with two more beads and the other sunscreens. Make sure that you use the same amount of sunscreen on each bead.
3. Place the fourth bead on the tray with no sunscreen as a control, or comparison, bead. Label this bead *control*.
4. Set the tray in the sun. Rate the beads according to color after one minute. A rating of one means the bead stayed completely white, while a rating of five is the darkest color possible (the control bead).
5. Leave the beads in the sun for one hour and rate them again. Record the data in a table.

* See page ii.

## New Zealand

**Use the map of New Zealand to answer the questions.**

1. On which island is the city of Christchurch located?

    a. South Island

    b. North Island

    c. Stewart Island

2. Gisborne is _____ of Dunedin.

    a. northeast

    b. northwest

    c. southeast

3. The capital of New Zealand is _____.

    a. Auckland

    b. Wellington

    c. New Plymouth

4. The distance between Greymouth and Christchurch is approximately _____.

    a. 150 kilometers

    b. 75 kilometers

    c. 300 kilometers

# BONUS

## Australia

**Use the map of Australia to answer the questions.**

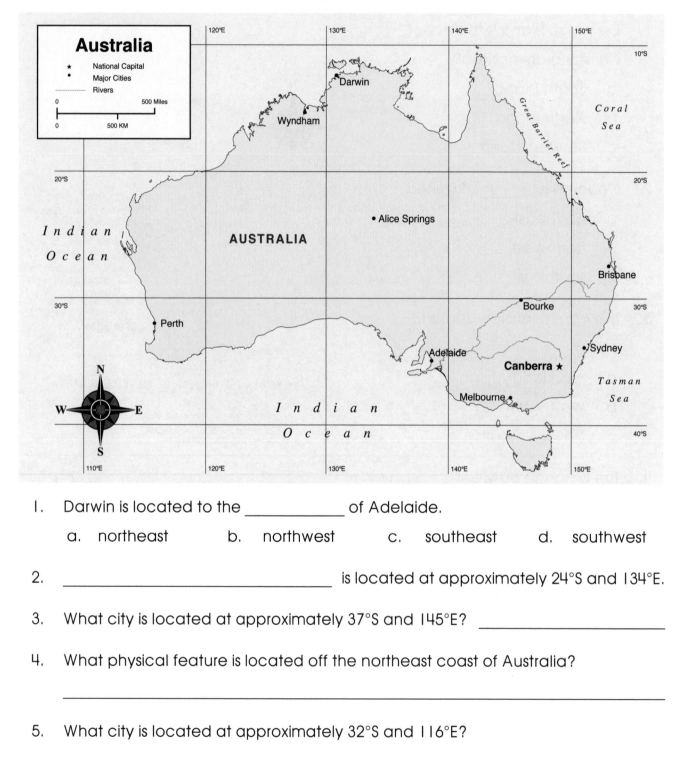

1. Darwin is located to the _____ of Adelaide.

   a. northeast      b. northwest      c. southeast      d. southwest

2. _____ is located at approximately 24°S and 134°E.

3. What city is located at approximately 37°S and 145°E? _____

4. What physical feature is located off the northeast coast of Australia?

   _____

5. What city is located at approximately 32°S and 116°E?

   _____

## Countries of Oceania

**Use the maps below to answer the questions.**

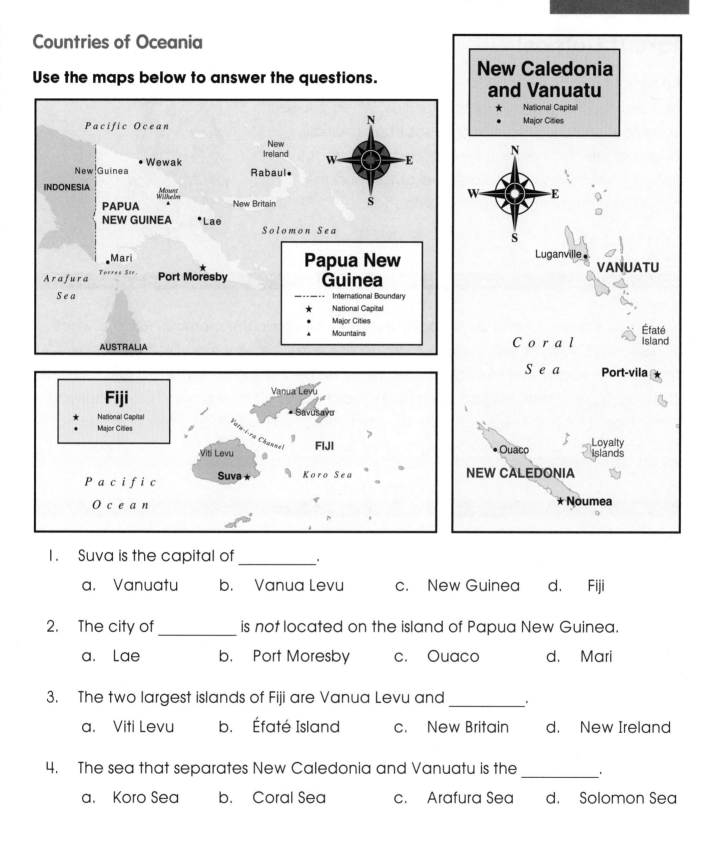

1. Suva is the capital of _____.

   a. Vanuatu     b. Vanua Levu     c. New Guinea     d. Fiji

2. The city of _____ is *not* located on the island of Papua New Guinea.

   a. Lae     b. Port Moresby     c. Ouaco     d. Mari

3. The two largest islands of Fiji are Vanua Levu and _____.

   a. Viti Levu     b. Éfaté Island     c. New Britain     d. New Ireland

4. The sea that separates New Caledonia and Vanuatu is the _____.

   a. Koro Sea     b. Coral Sea     c. Arafura Sea     d. Solomon Sea

**BONUS**

## Take It Outside!

Keep your math skills sharp this summer by taking advantage of calculation opportunities. When you see a number grouping, quickly add, subtract, multiply, or divide the numbers you see. For example, treat the first number on a license plate as a divisor and the remaining three numbers as the dividend.

Take a pen or pencil and a notebook outside with you in the morning. Record what you see and hear. Reflect on your morning observations. Make predictions of how things will look and sound at nighttime. What will be the same? What will be different? That night, go outside with an adult and record the sights and sounds. Compare your notes about day and night activity. How did your predictions compare to what you saw and heard at night? What might have caused your predictions to be different than what you observed?

Many animals rely on their sense of hearing to explore their environments. You can do the same thing on a summer afternoon. With an adult, sit in your backyard, on a park bench, or in some other safe and comfortable place. Open a notebook to a blank sheet of paper. With a pen or pencil, draw a star in the middle of the paper to represent yourself. Then, close your eyes and listen to the world around you. With your eyes closed, make small marks on the paper to describe the sounds you hear and the directions they are coming from. For example, you could draw a wavy line to represent the gurgling of a small stream or a swirl to represent the rush of wind through the trees. After a few minutes, open your eyes and examine your paper. How much could you tell about your surroundings just by listening?

* See page ii.

# Monthly Goals

Think of three goals to set for yourself this month. For example, you may want to read for 30 minutes each day. Write your goals on the lines and review them with an adult.

Place a sticker next to each goal that you complete. Feel proud that you have met your goals!

1. _____    PLACE STICKER HERE

2. _____    PLACE STICKER HERE

3. _____    PLACE STICKER HERE

# Word List

The following words are used in this section. They are good words for you to know. Read each word aloud. Use a dictionary to look up each word that you do not know. Then, write two sentences. Use a word from the word list in each sentence.

| | |
|---|---|
| chart | estimate |
| climate | symbol |
| compare | system |
| economy | temperature |

1. _____

   _____

2. _____

   _____

# Introduction to Endurance

## Physical Endurance

What do playing tag, jumping rope, and riding your bike have in common? They are all great ways to build endurance!

Having endurance means doing an activity for a long time before your body becomes tired. Your heart is stronger when you have endurance. Your muscles receive more oxygen.

Use the warm summer mornings and sunny days to go outside. Pick activities that you enjoy. Invite a family member on a walk or a bike ride. Play a game of basketball with friends. Leave the less active times for when it is dark, too hot, or raining.

Set an endurance goal this summer. For example, you might jump rope every day until you can jump for two minutes without stopping. Set new goals when you meet your old ones. Be proud of your endurance success!

## Endurance and Character Development

Showing mental endurance means sticking with something. You can show mental endurance every day. Staying with a task when you might want to quit and keeping at it until it is done are ways that you can show mental endurance.

Build your mental endurance this summer. Think of a time when you were frustrated or bored. Maybe you wanted to take swimming lessons. But, after a few early morning lessons, it is not as fun as you imagined. Think about some key points, such as how you asked all spring to take lessons. Be positive. Remind yourself that you have taken only a few lessons. You might get used to the early morning lessons. Think of ways to make the lessons more enjoyable, such as sleeping a few extra minutes during the morning car ride. Quitting should be the last option.

Build your mental endurance now. It will help prepare you for challenges you may face later!

## Add to find each sum.

**EXAMPLE:**
$$\frac{3}{4} + \frac{2}{4} = \frac{5}{4} \text{ or } 1\frac{1}{4}$$

1.  $\frac{6}{10} + \frac{8}{10} =$ _____

2.  $\frac{3}{4} + \frac{5}{4} =$ _____

3.  $\frac{9}{11} + \frac{2}{11} =$ _____

4.  $\frac{10}{12} + \frac{14}{12} =$ _____

5.  $\frac{6}{11} + \frac{7}{11} =$ _____

6.  $\frac{7}{12} + \frac{8}{12} =$ _____

7.  $\frac{6}{8} + \frac{5}{8} =$ _____

8.  $\frac{5}{15} + \frac{10}{15} =$ _____

9.  $\frac{9}{16} + \frac{9}{16} =$ _____

10.  $\frac{4}{7} + \frac{5}{7} =$ _____

11.  $\frac{8}{9} + \frac{6}{9} =$ _____

## Three Times the Fitness

A triathlon is an intense endurance race with swimming, cycling, and running events. This kind of athletic event requires incredible strength, flexibility, and endurance. Set up your own mini-triathlon to test your endurance. With an adult's help, plan a day where you can swim, bike, and run. For a variation, choose any three physical activities you prefer.

Try this activity several times throughout the summer. Start with short distances. Gradually increase the distance to build your stamina. Track your distance over the summer. How much farther were you able to travel by the end of August?

* See page ii.

## DAY 1

**Read the passage. Then, answer the questions.**

### Latitude and Longitude

Latitude and longitude lines divide the earth into regions. Latitude lines run around the globe from east to west. The line around the middle is called the equator. Latitude is measured using the equator as zero. The lines around the earth as you move north are either labeled with positive numbers or the letter *N* for north. The lines going south have either negative numbers or the letter *S* for south. Longitude lines run north to south from the north pole to the south pole. The zero point, or the Prime Meridian, for longitude runs through Greenwich, England. The numbers east of the Prime Meridian are either labeled with positive numbers or the letter *E* for east. The numbers west of the Prime Meridian are either labeled with negative numbers or the letter *W* for west. Both measurements are given in degrees. The latitude of Ottawa, the capital of Canada, is 45°25'0" N, which is read as "forty-five degrees, twenty-five minutes, zero seconds north." Latitude and longitude have long been used by people who study geography and mapmaking, as well as by explorers who travel around the world.

12.  What is the main idea of this passage?

    a.  Latitude and longitude lines are used to divide the earth into regions.

    b.  Longitude is measured in degrees.

    c.  The latitude of Ottawa is 45°25'0" N.

13.  Where is the zero point for longitude? _____

14.  Which people might use latitude and longitude most often? _____

_____

15.  Why do you think people might want to know their exact locations on the earth?

_____

_____

**FACTOID:** Some lungfish can survive out of the water for two years.

PLACE STICKER HERE

**Circle the electric circuit words in the puzzle. Words can go across and down.**

| current | closed circuit | negative | watts |
| metal | battery | positive | wires |
| insulator | conductor | voltage | resistance |

```
v  o  l  t  a  g  e  a  i  t  q  w  t  n
b  r  e  s  i  s  t  a  n  c  e  i  l  k
a  h  u  t  w  a  t  t  s  g  y  r  z  b
t  e  c  g  j  m  d  x  u  q  k  e  e  v
t  y  o  f  h  v  k  u  l  z  b  s  r  h
e  f  n  r  o  w  g  d  a  a  q  a  z  x
r  u  d  h  n  b  v  f  t  r  e  w  n  s
y  j  u  y  u  i  j  m  o  k  i  o  e  p
z  i  c  q  w  c  u  r  r  e  n  t  g  l
p  g  t  a  m  z  x  s  e  d  c  v  a  m
c  l  o  s  e  d  c  i  r  c  u  i  t  j
b  g  r  t  t  y  h  n  m  j  u  o  i  u
o  l  p  m  a  q  p  o  s  i  t  i  v  e
h  y  u  j  l  w  r  y  i  p  k  h  e  f
```

# DAY 2

**Subtract to find each difference.**

**EXAMPLE:**

$$\frac{4}{5} - \frac{1}{5} = \frac{3}{5}$$ ← subtract the numerators
← keep the same denominator

1. $\frac{2}{6} - \frac{1}{6} =$

2. $\frac{5}{10} - \frac{3}{10} =$

3. $\frac{3}{4} - \frac{2}{4} =$

4. $6\frac{8}{10}$
  $-3\frac{4}{10}$

5. $8\frac{4}{10}$
  $-3\frac{3}{10}$

6. $7\frac{2}{15}$
  $-3\frac{1}{15}$

---

**Use editing marks to correct the punctuation and capitalization in the letter.**

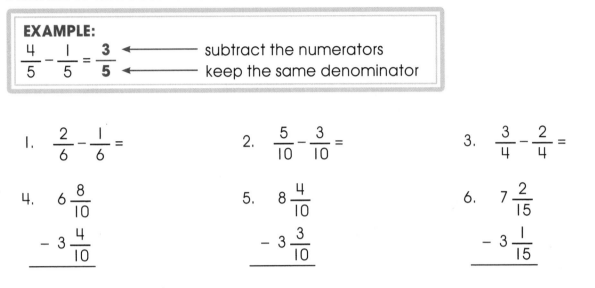

july 17 2015

dear david

thank you for sending me the pictures

from your trip it looks like you had a great

time do you want me to send them back

next week im going to kansas city with

my dad i can't wait

your friend

greg

**FITNESS FLASH:** Jog in place for 30 seconds.

* See page ii.

PLACE
STICKER
HERE

**Solve each problem.**

1.      5,162
     − 2,168

2.      9,252
     − 5,003

3.      7,825
     − 3,148

4.      3,529
     + 7,506

5.      8,929
     + 4,050

6.      9,341
     − 6,037

7.      2,629
     + 7,536

8.      4,528
     + 1,257

9.      7,932
     − 5,847

10.     9,826
     + 1,329

11.     4,723
     + 5,297

12.     3,872
     − 1,799

**Write a letter to a friend, a grandparent, or someone else of your choice. Make sure your letter contains all five parts of a letter.**

_____

_____

_____

_____

_____

_____

_____

_____

# DAY 3

**Read the passage. Then, answer the questions.**

## Political Parties

Political parties are groups of people who feel the same way about one or more issues. Each party may work to elect several candidates to office, from city mayor to the president of the United States. Political parties often use symbols to represent themselves. When people see the symbols, they think of the political parties. The donkey was first used in a political advertisement to represent President Andrew Jackson, who was with the U.S. Democratic Party. Donkeys are considered smart and courageous. The U.S. Republican Party symbol is the elephant. Elephants are known for their strength and intelligence. Both of these parties use red, white, and blue—the colors of the U.S. flag. Many of the Canadian political parties have maple leaves as part of their logos or designs to indicate that the parties are tied to their country. The maple leaf appears on the Canadian flag. Political parties in Great Britain use different symbols. The Labour Party uses the rose (the national flower), the Conservative Party uses the oak tree (for strength), and the Liberal Democrats use a dove (for peace).

13. What is the main idea of this passage?

    a. When people see a symbol, they think of a political party.

    b. Political parties use symbols to represent them.

    c. The Canadian flag has a maple leaf on it.

14. What are political parties? _____

_____

15. Why do you think a political party might use symbols from its country's flag?

_____

_____

16. What symbols are used by British political parties? _____

**FACTOID:** A group of frogs is called an army.

104

**Use the information below to convert each measurement.**

| 16 ounces = 1 pound | 2,000 pounds = 1 ton |
|---|---|

1. 160 ounces = _____ pounds
2. _____ ounces = 5 pounds
3. 5 tons = _____ pounds
4. _____ ounces = 9 pounds
5. 4,000 pounds = _____ tons
6. _____ pounds = 7 tons
7. 8,000 pounds = _____ tons
8. _____ ounces = 11 pounds
9. _____ pounds = 3 tons
10. 10 tons = _____ pounds
11. 32 ounces = _____ pounds
12. _____ ounces = 3 pounds

**Use the suffixes and base words to create as many words as you can.**

| Suffixes | | | | |
|---|---|---|---|---|
| -er | -ful | -less | -ly | -ness |

| Base Words | | | | | |
|---|---|---|---|---|---|
| teach | thought | beauty | boast | cheer | hope |
| wonder | bake | play | care | doubt | shy |
| awkward | help | peace | law | quick | friend |

_____     _____     _____

_____     _____     _____

_____     _____     _____

_____     _____     _____

## DAY 4

**Write the correct word(s) to complete each sentence.**

| water | calcium | circulatory | cells | iron | digestive |
|-------|---------|-------------|-------|------|-----------|

13. The human body is made up of millions of tiny _____ .

14. The human body is mostly _____, between 55 and 75 percent.

15. The human body has many metals and minerals in it, two of which are

    _____ and _____ .

16. The salivary glands, esophagus, stomach, gallbladder, large intestines, and

    small intestines are part of the _____ system.

17. The _____ system moves blood throughout the body.

**Using a thesaurus, write one synonym and one antonym for each word.**

|  | **Synonym** | **Antonym** |
|--|-------------|-------------|
| 18. rough | _____ | _____ |
| 19. problem | _____ | _____ |
| 20. interesting | _____ | _____ |
| 21. surprise | _____ | _____ |
| 22. happy | _____ | _____ |
| 23. harvest | _____ | _____ |

**FITNESS FLASH:** Hop on your right foot for 30 seconds.

* See page ii.

PLACE STICKER HERE

**Use the chart to answer each question.**

## Popular Joke Web Sites

| Web Site | Number of Visitors |
|---|---|
| ruhilarious.joke | 83,121 |
| lapsincomedy.joke | 58,452 |
| webofpuns.joke | 70,907 |
| quietquippers.joke | 46,162 |
| dropmeapunchline.joke | 49,323 |

1. Which Web site was the least popular? _____

2. Which Web site was the most popular? _____

3. How many more visitors did the most popular site receive than the least

   popular site? _____

4. How many more visitors did *webofpuns.joke* receive than *lapsincomedy.joke*?

   _____

5. How many fewer visitors did *dropmeapunchline.joke* receive than

   *lapsincomedy.joke*? _____

6. What is the average number of people who visited these Web sites? To find the

   average, divide the total number of visitors by the number of Web sites.

   _____

# DAY 5

**Read the passage. Then, answer the questions.**

## Reading Maps

Have you ever used a map to plan a route? A world map shows the outlines of the continents and seas. It may have parts shaded brown and green to show areas of desert or forest. A city map shows important buildings, such as the library or city hall, as well as city streets. Maps use symbols to help you understand them. A compass rose looks like an eight-pointed star inside a circle. It shows you the directions north, south, east, and west. North is usually at the top. A map scale tells you how the distances on a map relate to the real world. For example, one inch (2.5 cm) on the map may be equal to 100 miles (160.9 km). A map legend shows you what other symbols mean. A black dot may stand for a city, a star inside a circle may mean a country's capital city, and an airplane may be used to represent an airport. Knowing what these symbols mean makes it much easier to travel.

7.  What is the main idea of this passage?

    a.   Some maps use a compass rose and a scale.

    b.   A world map is very different from a city map.

    c.   Maps use symbols to help you understand them.

8.  What does a world map show? _____

    _____

9.  What does a city map show? _____

    _____

10. What does a compass rose show?_____

    _____

**CHARACTER CHECK:** What is the golden rule? On a separate sheet of paper, explain the rule using your own words.

PLACE STICKER HERE

**Write the missing syllable(s) for each word. The stressed syllable is shown. Then, write the entire word.**

| busy | violin | begin | bacon | unlock | into |
|------|--------|-------|-------|--------|------|
| accept | ~~parent~~ | dial | salad | table | depend |

**EXAMPLE:**

'par **e n t**    **parent**        1.  'in ___ ___        _____

2.  ___ ___ 'pend        _____        3.  'ba ___ ___ ___        _____

4.  'di ___ ___        _____        5.  ___ ___ 'gin        _____

6.  'sal ___ ___        _____        7.  ___ ___ 'lock        _____

8.  'ta ___ ___ ___        _____        9.  ___ ___ ___ 'lin        _____

10.  ___ ___ 'cept        _____        11.  'bus ___        _____

**Write a self-portrait poem.**

Write your name.

Write two words that describe you.

Write three words that tell what you like to do.

Write two more words that describe you.

Write your name again.

_____

_____

_____

_____

_____

# DAY 6

**Read the passage. Then, answer the questions.**

## U.S. State Symbols

The United States has many national symbols that represent liberty and freedom. Each U.S. state also has its own symbols, including a state animal, a state flower, and a state flag. The state of Washington has a picture of George Washington, the first U.S. president, on its flag. The state fruit is the apple, and the state vegetable is the Walla Walla sweet onion, which grows in the city of Walla Walla. Louisiana has its state bird, the pelican, on its flag. The state reptile is the alligator. Alaska's flag shows a pattern of stars known as the Big Dipper. The state fish is the king salmon, and the state mineral is gold. Ohio's state insect is the ladybug. The state tree is the buckeye, and the state beverage is tomato juice. The state plant of Texas is the prickly pear cactus, and the state flower is the bluebonnet. Each state's symbols can tell you a lot about the plants and the animals that live there.

12.  What is the main idea of this passage?

    a.  National symbols represent liberty and freedom.

    b.  U.S. states have many different symbols.

    c.  The state tree of Ohio is the buckeye.

13.  What are the state bird and the state reptile of Louisiana? _____

_____

14.  What does the state of Alaska's flag look like? _____

_____

15.  The Walla Walla sweet onion is the state vegetable of which state?

_____

**FACTOID:** Dragonflies can fly at speeds of up to 40 miles (64 km) per hour.

**Fractions that have a denominator of 10 can also be written as decimals. Write each fraction and/or decimal.**

**EXAMPLE:**

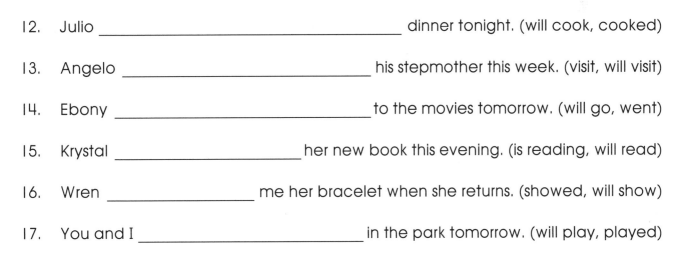

$\dfrac{6}{10}$ or **0.6**

1. _____ or _____

2. _____ or _____

3. _____ or _____

4. _____ or _____

5. _____ or _____

6. $\dfrac{3}{10}$ or _____

7. $1\dfrac{7}{10}$ or _____

8. $3\dfrac{5}{10}$ or _____

9. 1.9 or _____

10. 0.8 or _____

11. 3.4 or _____

**Write the future-tense verb from the parentheses to complete each sentence.**

12. Julio _____ dinner tonight. (will cook, cooked)

13. Angelo _____ his stepmother this week. (visit, will visit)

14. Ebony _____ to the movies tomorrow. (will go, went)

15. Krystal _____ her new book this evening. (is reading, will read)

16. Wren _____ me her bracelet when she returns. (showed, will show)

17. You and I _____ in the park tomorrow. (will play, played)

# DAY 7

**An analogy is a comparison between two word pairs. Complete each analogy.**

**EXAMPLE:** Story is to read as song is to _____ *sing* _____ .

18. Brother is to boy as sister is to _____ .

19. Princess is to queen as prince is to _____ .

20. Milk is to drink as hamburger is to _____ .

21. Daisy is to flower as maple is to _____ .

22. Car is to driver as plane is to _____ .

23. Ceiling is to room as lid is to _____ .

24. Paper is to tear as glass is to _____ .

**Make a list of five or six activities you like to do. Some examples are running, hopping, sit-ups, jumping jacks, touching your toes, push-ups, skipping rope, and playing sports. Write about how these activities help you stay healthy.**

_____

_____

_____

_____

_____

_____

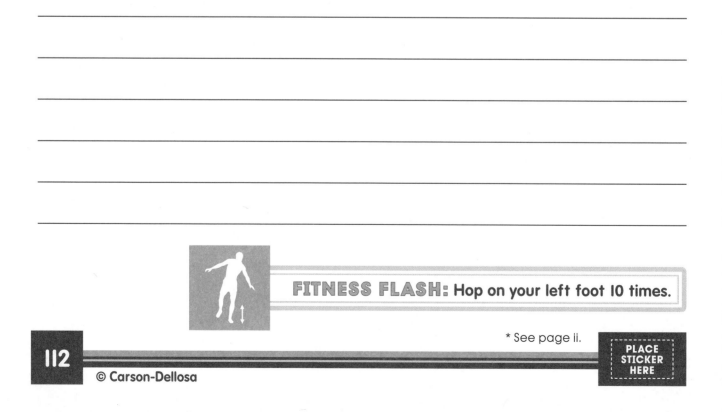

**FITNESS FLASH:** Hop on your left foot 10 times.

\* See page ii.

PLACE STICKER HERE

When a whole object is divided into 100 equal parts, each part is one hundredth ($\frac{1}{100}$ or 0.01). Write each fraction as a decimal.

**EXAMPLE:**
$$\frac{49}{100} = \underline{0} \cdot \underline{49}$$

1. $\frac{25}{100} = \underline{\quad} \cdot \underline{\quad}$

2. $\frac{20}{100} = \underline{\quad} \cdot \underline{\quad}$

3. $\frac{86}{100} = \underline{\quad} \cdot \underline{\quad}$

4. $\frac{37}{100} = \underline{\quad} \cdot \underline{\quad}$

5. $\frac{9}{100} = \underline{\quad} \cdot \underline{\quad}$

**Write each mixed number as a decimal.**

6. $1\frac{93}{100} = \underline{\quad} \cdot \underline{\quad}$

7. $7\frac{15}{100} = \underline{\quad} \cdot \underline{\quad}$

8. $15\frac{47}{100} = \underline{\quad} \cdot \underline{\quad}$

9. $46\frac{89}{100} = \underline{\quad} \cdot \underline{\quad}$

10. $35\frac{6}{100} = \underline{\quad} \cdot \underline{\quad}$

11. $625\frac{12}{100} = \underline{\quad} \cdot \underline{\quad}$

**Circle each adjective. Then, write the noun or the pronoun that is being described.**

A (beautiful) light flashed across the (cloudy) sky. *light , sky*

12. On the tall mountain, we found blue and yellow flowers. _____

13. He was stronger after he chopped the wood. _____

14. It is fun and exciting to go sledding. _____

**Complete each sentence using adjectives.**

15. My_____ pencil is never at my desk.

16. The _____ students were having a _____ time.

17. The _____ , _____ ride was making me dizzy.

# DAY 8

**Read the story. Then, list three events that happened.**

### Who Did It?

Grayson and Dustin were playing volleyball in Dustin's backyard with some other friends. They had been playing all afternoon in the hot sun. Dustin decided that he was tired of playing volleyball. He sat down on the back steps to watch the others. "I am very thirsty," Dustin said. "I'm going into the house to get a drink of water." Several of the others decided that they were thirsty too, and they went inside with Dustin. "Wait for me!" shouted Grayson. "I'm coming too!"

The boys who went inside decided to play a game instead of playing volleyball. Then, the other boys thought they had better go home because it was close to dinnertime. Dustin said that he was hungry and went to the kitchen for something to eat. Grayson ran after him to remind him that his mom said that they were not supposed to eat anything before dinner. Then, Dustin's dad came into the kitchen to make dinner. "Who ate all of the hot dogs?" he exclaimed. "They were right here on the counter."

Grayson and Dustin looked at each other. "We didn't, Dad," Dustin said. Dad said, "Well, somebody must have. Do you have any clues?"

They all started looking around for clues. The boys' muddy shoes had left tracks on the floor, but the tracks weren't in the area where the hot dogs had been. After they looked around the kitchen, they sat down to discuss "the case of the missing hot dogs." Then, everyone heard what sounded like a satisfied *meow* coming from the den. They rushed into the den just in time to see Tiger, Dustin's cat, gobbling down the last hot dog. Tiger licked his paws clean. "No wonder we didn't find any cat tracks in the kitchen," laughed Dustin's dad. "Tiger always keeps his paws very clean, unlike some boys I know."

18. _____

19. _____

20. _____

**FACTOID:** The amount of water pouring over Niagara Falls each second could fill 13,000 bathtubs.

**Use the graph to answer each question.**

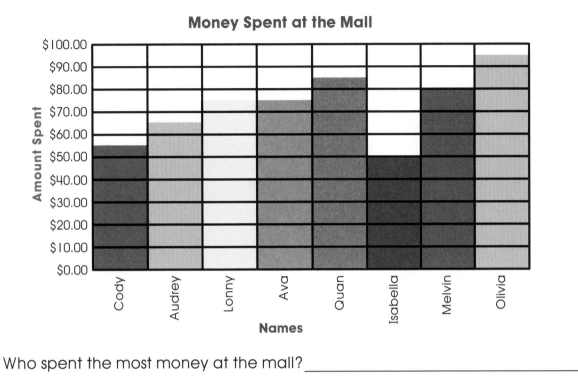

**Money Spent at the Mall**

1. Who spent the most money at the mall? _____

2. Who spent the least money at the mall? _____

3. How much more money did Melvin spend than Cody? _____

4. How much less money did Audrey spend than Olivia? _____

5. Which shoppers spent the same amount of money? _____

6. What was the average amount of money spent? To find the average, divide the total amount spent by the number of shoppers. _____

**Circle each root word. Underline each prefix.**

7. unhappy

8. preheat

9. bicycle

10. review

11. misunderstand

12. unknown

13. uncover

14. uniform

15. replace

# DAY 9

**Solve each problem.**

**EXAMPLES:**

```
    $57.34
  + 62.89
  $120.23
```

```
    $62.89
  − 34.91
   $27.98
```

```
    $12.45
  ×      3
   $37.35
```

```
        $3.95
  5)$19.75
     −15
       47
      −45
       25
      −25
        0
```

16.
```
    $409.75
  − 249.83
  $      .
```

17.
```
    $14.74
  ×      3
  $    .
```

18.
```
    $492.00
  − 349.50
  $      .
```

19.
```
     $    .
  4)$12.92
```

20.
```
    $162.49
  + 186.32
  $      .
```

21.
```
     $    .
  7)$49.77
```

22.
```
    $601.89
  + 403.23
  $      .
```

23.
```
    $9.57
  ×      6
  $    .
```

**Write a noun to go with the adjectives.**

**EXAMPLE:** two red _apples_

25. fluffy, yellow _____

27. cold, wet _____

29. dark, strange _____

31. wild, dangerous _____

24. fancy, little _____

26. small, pink _____

28. smooth, green _____

30. fat, juicy _____

32. loud, shrill _____

**FITNESS FLASH:** Do 10 jumping jacks.

\* See page ii.

PLACE STICKER HERE

**Write the correct word to complete each sentence.**

| energy | food groups | Nutrients |
|---|---|---|
| Exercise | healthy | water |

1. _____ are basic, nourishing ingredients in good foods that you eat.

2. _____helps you strengthen your muscles, heart, and lungs.

3. Your body is between 55 and 75 percent _____.

4. Meat, fruits, vegetables, milk, and breads and cereals make up the basic _____.

5. Being healthy means feeling good and having the_____ to work and play.

6. Being _____ means feeling good and staying well.

**Add both a prefix and a suffix to each word.**

7. _____ print_____ 8. _____ port_____

9. _____ spell_____ 10. _____ courage _____

11. _____ light_____ 12. _____ cook_____

13. _____ lock_____ 14. _____ agree_____

**Choose two of the new words and use them in sentences.**

15. _____

16. _____

# DAY 10

To find the product of multiples of 10 or 100, find the product of the basic fact and then count the zeros in the factors. Solve each problem and write how many zeros are in the answer.

$10 \times 8 = 80$ ( 1 zero)    $10 \times 80 = 800$ (2 zeros)    $10 \times 800 = 8,000$ (3 zeros)

17.  $7 \times 100 =$ _____    18.  $39 \times 10 =$ _____    19.  $30 \times 300 =$ _____

20.   900
    $\times$ 40

21.   600
    $\times$ 10

22.   230
    $\times$ 20

23.   700
    $\times$ 80

24.   5,000
    $\times$   50

25.   600
    $\times$ 90

26.   4,400
    $\times$   30

27.   7,000
    $\times$   60

---

Add *-er* and *-est* to make each adjective comparative and superlative.

|  | -er | -est |
|---|---|---|
| 28.  red | _____ | _____ |
| 29.  hot | _____ | _____ |
| 30.  nice | _____ | _____ |

**CHARACTER CHECK:** What is the hardest thing that you have ever done? How did it make you feel? On a separate sheet of paper, write a paragraph about your experience.

PLACE STICKER HERE

**Use the place value chart to write each number.**

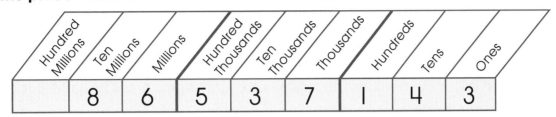

| Hundred Millions | Ten Millions | Millions | Hundred Thousands | Ten Thousands | Thousands | Hundreds | Tens | Ones |
|---|---|---|---|---|---|---|---|---|
| | 8 | 6 | 5 | 3 | 7 | 1 | 4 | 3 |

**EXAMPLE:**

Eighty-six million five hundred thirty-seven thousand one hundred forty-three

_____ **86,537,143** _____

1. One million three hundred sixty-nine thousand _____

2. Five hundred two million one hundred thousand seven _____

3. 375,403,101 _____

_____

4. 894,336,045 _____

_____

**The word *and* is often used too frequently in writing. Rewrite this run-on sentence, leaving out the word *and* as much as possible.**

My friend and I visited Cardiff, Wales, and we learned that Cardiff is the capital and largest port of Wales and the city lies on the River Taff near the Bristol Channel and Cardiff is near the largest coal mines in Great Britain.

_____

_____

_____

# DAY 11

**Read the passage. Then, answer the questions.**

## Plant Parts

Plants have many parts. You can see some of them, but they have parts that you can't see too. The plant begins with the root system underground. It sends out roots into the soil to gather water and minerals. The part of the plant that grows out of the ground is called the stem. The stem moves water and minerals from the soil into the leaves. The leaves use sunlight, air, water, and minerals to make food for the plant, which is then moved to other parts of the plant. The leaves also produce the oxygen we breathe. Some leaves have only broad, flat areas connected to the stems. Others have many leaflets, or slim, needle-like parts. Many plants have flowers on top of the stems. The petals of the flowers help attract bees and butterflies, which bring pollen from other flowers. The pollen helps flowers make new plants for the next year. Some plants bear fruit. New plants can grow from the seeds in the fruit.

5. What is the main idea of this passage?

    a. A plant's root system is underground.

    b. Plants have parts such as roots, leaves, and petals.

    c. Bees and butterflies like flowers.

6. How does the root system help the plant? _____

_____

7. What do leaves need to make food for the plant? _____

_____

8. How do the petals of a flower help the plant? _____

_____

_____

**FACTOID:** Benjamin Franklin started the first lending library.

PLACE
STICKER
HERE

**Multiply to find each product.**

1. $\begin{array}{r} 39 \\ \times\ 69 \\ \hline \end{array}$

2. $\begin{array}{r} 72 \\ \times\ 18 \\ \hline \end{array}$

3. $\begin{array}{r} 85 \\ \times\ 36 \\ \hline \end{array}$

4. $\begin{array}{r} 23 \\ \times\ 87 \\ \hline \end{array}$

5. $\begin{array}{r} 46 \\ \times\ 77 \\ \hline \end{array}$

6. $\begin{array}{r} 57 \\ \times\ 49 \\ \hline \end{array}$

7. $\begin{array}{r} 41 \\ \times\ 73 \\ \hline \end{array}$

8. $\begin{array}{r} 48 \\ \times\ 95 \\ \hline \end{array}$

9. $\begin{array}{r} 88 \\ \times\ 66 \\ \hline \end{array}$

10. $\begin{array}{r} 68 \\ \times\ 92 \\ \hline \end{array}$

**Write S for the word pairs that are synonyms, A for the word pairs that are antonyms, and H for the word pairs that are homophones.**

**EXAMPLE:**

| | |
|---|---|
| tie • bind | *S* |
| high • low | *a* |
| here • hear | *H* |

11. weep • cry _____

12. wonderful • terrible _____

13. look • stare _____

14. huge • large _____

15. away • toward _____

16. walk • stroll _____

17. never • always _____

18. bear • bare _____

19. ask • tell _____

20. cymbal • symbol _____

21. many • numerous _____

22. end • begin _____

23. hair • hare _____

24. move • transport _____

25. problem • solution _____

26. idea • thought _____

27. claws • clause _____

28. I'll • isle _____

**Choose four idioms and draw a picture for each one.**

- Could you lend a hand?
- The boys were shooting the breeze.
- She has a bee in her bonnet.
- She slept like a log.
- I got it straight from the horse's mouth.
- You won the game by the skin of your teeth.

- Time flies.
- Keep a stiff upper lip.
- She's a ball of fire.
- I'd really like to catch her eye.
- I was dog tired.

**FITNESS FLASH:** Jog in place for 30 seconds.

* See page ii.

PLACE
STICKER
HERE

**The words below are often misspelled. First, write each word in cursive. Next, write each word using your opposite hand. Then, write the mirror image of each word.**

|  | | Cursive | Opposite Hand | Mirror Image |
|---|---|---|---|---|
| 1. | although | _____ | _____ | _____ |
| 2. | believe | _____ | _____ | _____ |
| 3. | trouble | _____ | _____ | _____ |
| 4. | bought | _____ | _____ | _____ |
| 5. | chocolate | _____ | _____ | _____ |
| 6. | aunt | _____ | _____ | _____ |
| 7. | friend | _____ | _____ | _____ |

**Complete the table below for the members of your family. Include aunts, uncles, and cousins. List each person's age, height, eye color, and hair color.**

| Family Member | Age | Height | Eye Color | Hair Color |
|---|---|---|---|---|
|  |  |  |  |  |
|  |  |  |  |  |
|  |  |  |  |  |
|  |  |  |  |  |
|  |  |  |  |  |
|  |  |  |  |  |
|  |  |  |  |  |
|  |  |  |  |  |

**Read the passage. Then, answer the questions.**

## Climate

The climate describes the weather in an area over a long period of time. If you live somewhere where it rains a lot, then you live in a rainy climate. If your town is very hot and dry, then you may live in a desert climate. Some cities, such as San Diego, California, have a very mild climate. Others, such as New Orleans, Louisiana, have warm, heavy air, so it is humid most of the time. Although the weather in a place may change from day to day, a region's climate seldom changes. Factors other than weather can also affect the climate. Areas that are close to the sea tend to be cooler and wetter. They may also be cloudy because clouds form when warm inland air meets the cooler air from the sea. Mountains may also affect climate. Because the temperature at the top of a mountain is cooler than at ground level, it may snow year-round. Regions near Earth's equator, or middle, are warmer than those at the poles. Sunlight must travel farther to get to the north and south poles, so these areas are much colder.

8. What is the main idea of this passage?

   a. Climate is the weather in a place over a long period of time.

   b. The north and south poles are very cold.

   c. Some climates are rainy, and some are very hot.

9. How are the climates in San Diego and New Orleans different? _____

   _____

10. What is the difference between weather and climate? _____

   _____

11. How are climates near the equator different from those at the poles? _____

   _____

**FACTOID:** Recycling a ton of paper saves about 24 trees.

PLACE STICKER HERE

**Divide to find each quotient.**

**EXAMPLE:**

```
      2 R8
  20)48
   -40
     8
```

1. 30)189

2. 70)456

3. 80)504

4. 30)281

5. 60)246

6. 90)458

7. 60)573

8. 40)172

9. 80)410

10. 60)692

11. 70)661

**Write about your favorite folktale. Tell how the story begins, what happens in the middle, and how it ends. Write it in your own words and in the correct order. Do not write the whole story.**

_____

_____

_____

_____

_____

_____

# DAY 14

**Read the passage. Then, answer the questions.**

### Biofuels

Gasoline is used in cars, and oil is used to heat many homes. Biofuels have similar uses, but they are made from things like vegetable oil, which can be recycled and used again. Diesel is a type of fuel similar to heating oil. Diesel fuel is used in some cars and trucks. Biodiesel, most of which is made from soybean oil, burns more cleanly than diesel. It can be used in diesel engines without having to add any special parts. Biodiesel produces less pollution, so it is better for the environment. Gasoline is known as a fossil fuel, which means it comes from layers deep inside the earth that are made up of plants and animals that lived millions of years ago. Biofuel comes from plants we grow today, so it is a renewable resource. Some biofuels are created from restaurants' leftover oil that was used to cook french fries or fried chicken. Instead of throwing the oil away, some people are using it to run their cars!

12. What is the main idea of this passage?

    a. Biofuels are better for the environment than fossil fuels.

    b. Gasoline and diesel are used to run cars.

    c. Some people throw away the oil they have used for cooking.

13. What are biofuels? _____

    _____

14. What is a fossil fuel?

    a. a material that flowers produce

    b. oil used to make fried foods

    c. a fuel made from plants and animals that lived long ago

**FITNESS FLASH: Hop on your right foot for 30 seconds.**

* See page ii.

PLACE STICKER HERE

**Classify each triangle as equilateral, isosceles, or scalene.**

> **Equilateral Triangle:** three congruent sides
> **Isosceles Triangle:** two congruent sides
> **Scalene Triangle:** no congruent sides

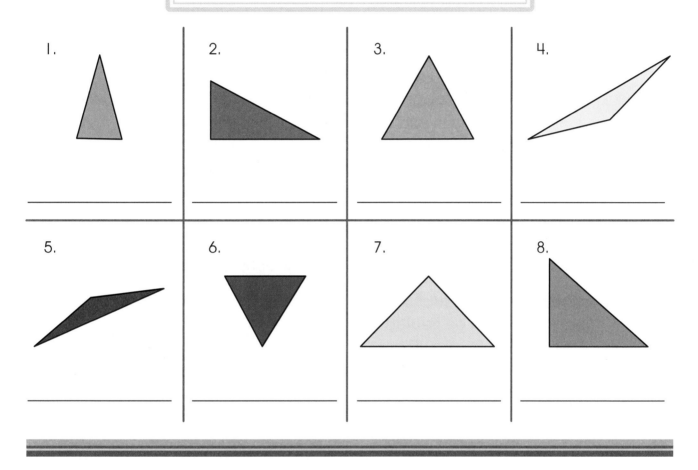

1. _____

2. _____

3. _____

4. _____

5. _____

6. _____

7. _____

8. _____

**Write an adverb to describe each verb.**

**EXAMPLE:**

walk _____*quietly*_____

9. burned _____

10. smiled _____

11. arrived _____

12. painted _____

13. went _____

14. laughed _____

15. folded _____

**Read the passage. Then, answer the questions.**

### Citizens' Rights and Responsibilities

In Canada and the United States, citizens have certain rights. These rights are often a part of the country's laws. American and Canadian citizens who are age 18 and over are given the right to vote. Citizens of the United States and Canada also have the right to a fair trial and the right to speak freely about what they believe. They can practice any religion they want to, and they have the right to gather peacefully to exchange ideas. They have the right to ask their government to change laws that they think are wrong. With these rights come responsibilities too. People should obey the laws of their country. They should respect the opinions of others, even if they disagree with them. They should help others in their community and try to protect their environment. It is important to remember that all citizens are a part of a large community and that everyone deserves to be treated fairly.

16. What is the main idea of this passage?

    a. All citizens of a country have rights and responsibilities.

    b. Citizens have the right to vote.

    c. Everyone should be treated fairly in a community.

17. What are three responsibilities citizens have? _____

_____

18. At least how old must citizens be to vote in Canada and the United States?

_____

19. What are three rights that citizens have in Canada and the United States?

_____

_____

**CHARACTER CHECK:** Think of three things that you like about yourself. Write these characteristics on a sheet of paper and post it where you will see it often.

**Multiply dollar amounts like whole numbers. Then, the decimal point is inserted two numbers from the right to show cents. Multiply to find each product.**

**EXAMPLE:**

$$\begin{array}{r} \$0.24 \\ \times\ \ 89 \\ \hline 216 \\ +\ 1920 \\ \hline 2136 \end{array}$$

$24 \times 9 = 216$

$24 \times 80 = 1920$

$1920 + 216 = 2136$

Place the decimal and dollar sign: **$21.36**

1.  $$\begin{array}{r} \$0.65 \\ \times\ \ 24 \end{array}$$

2.  $$\begin{array}{r} \$0.52 \\ \times\ \ 36 \end{array}$$

3.  $$\begin{array}{r} \$0.94 \\ \times\ \ 13 \end{array}$$

4.  $$\begin{array}{r} \$0.45 \\ \times\ \ 25 \end{array}$$

5.  $$\begin{array}{r} \$0.81 \\ \times\ \ 34 \end{array}$$

6.  $$\begin{array}{r} \$0.59 \\ \times\ \ 54 \end{array}$$

7.  $$\begin{array}{r} \$3.52 \\ \times\ \ 34 \end{array}$$

8.  $$\begin{array}{r} \$3.45 \\ \times\ \ 56 \end{array}$$

**The perimeter is the distance around an object. Measure the length of each side to find the perimeter in centimeters.**

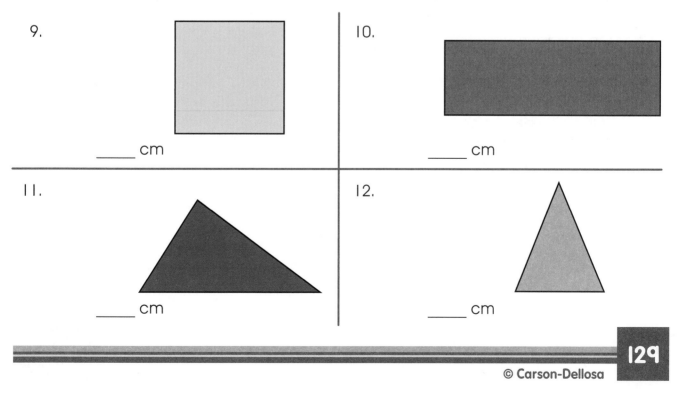

9. _____ cm

10. _____ cm

11. _____ cm

12. _____ cm

# DAY 16

**Write the definition of each term. Then, draw an example of each.**

13. segment _____

    _____

14. intersecting lines _____

    _____

15. parallel lines _____

    _____

16. perimeter _____

    _____

**Write whether each underlined adverb tells where, how, or when.**

17. Animals are <u>sometimes</u> pets. _____

18. We saw a huge truck on the freeway <u>yesterday</u>. _____

19. Joe <u>quickly</u> ran to catch the bus. _____

20. We could hear the sound <u>far</u> below us. _____

21. Our campfire burned <u>brightly</u> all night. _____

22. We are going <u>there</u> next winter. _____

**FACTOID:** An ostrich's eye is bigger than its brain.

PLACE
STICKER
HERE

## Loyalty Lunch

Loyalty means to support and stand up for the people you love. Think of the characteristics that make a person loyal. Then, design a menu for a loyalty lunch to share with a friend or family member. Think of a special name that uses a characteristic of loyalty for each food item, such as Dependable Diced Tomatoes or Honest Olives. Gather some ingredients for the meal. Use folded index cards to make place cards and labels that tell what each food is. As you eat, talk to your dining partner about why you appreciate his loyal friendship.

**Circle the best definition of each underlined word.**

1.  Can you <u>solve</u> this problem?

    a.  copy              b.  answer              c.  recall

2.  Make an <u>estimate</u> of how many people live in the United States.

    a.  guess              b.  tally              c.  rank

3.  Will you <u>complete</u> your test in 10 minutes?

    a.  support              b.  use              c.  finish

4.  Do <u>sections</u> 1 and 2 on this page.

    a.  groups              b.  parts              c.  chapters

# DAY 17

**Write the definition of each term. Then, draw an example of each.**

5.  congruent figures _____

    _____

6.  right angle _____

    _____

7.  triangle _____

    _____

8.  parallelogram _____

    _____

---

| 1 pint (pt.) is equal to 2 cups | 1 gallon (gal.) is equal to 4 quarts. |
|---|---|
| 1 quart (qt.) is equal to 2 pints. | 1 pound (lb.) is equal to 16 ounces. |

**Circle the best answer.**

| 9. | The capacity of a glass | 2 cups | 2 pt. | 2 qt. | 2 gal. |
|---|---|---|---|---|---|
| 10. | The capacity of a bathtub | 60 cups | 60 pt. | 60 qt. | 60 gal. |
| 11. | The capacity of a kitchen sink | 2 cups | 2 pt. | 2 qt. | 2 gal. |

**Convert each measurement.**

12.  5 pt. = _____ cups      13.  4 pt. = _____ qt.      14.  2 qt. = _____ pt.

15.  32 oz. = _____ lb.      16.  3 gal. = _____ qt.      17.  8 cups = _____ pt.

**FITNESS FLASH:** Hop on your left foot 10 times.

* See page ii.

PLACE STICKER HERE

**Find a recipe. List the ingredients. Estimate the price of each ingredient. Then, go to a store and record the actual price of each ingredient. Compare your estimated and actual prices.**

| | Ingredient | Estimated Price | Actual Price |
|---|---|---|---|
| 1. | _____ | _____ | _____ |
| 2. | _____ | _____ | _____ |
| 3. | _____ | _____ | _____ |
| 4. | _____ | _____ | _____ |
| 5. | _____ | _____ | _____ |
| 6. | _____ | _____ | _____ |

**An event can cause another event to happen. A clue word can help you find out which is the cause and which is the effect. In each sentence, underline the cause with a straight line ( ___ ) and underline the effect with a dashed line ( _ _ _ _ ). Draw a box around each clue word.**

**EXAMPLE:** The flowers were very bright, so they attracted a lot of butterflies.

7. The book was ripped because the dog chewed it.

8. Because it was so cold, Betty could ice-skate for only a short while.

9. I went to bed early last night because I was so tired.

10. Because it was raining hard, we couldn't play outside.

11. The rabbit ran away quickly because she saw a cat.

12. It was very foggy outside, so we could not see the mountains.

13. Because we got to the camp too late, there was no time for hiking.

# DAY 18

**Read the passage. Then, answer the questions.**

## The Economy

You may have heard your family or a newscaster discuss the economy. The economy is a system in which goods and services are exchanged for money. Goods are items that are produced, such as books and clothing. Services are activities that people do for each other. For example, a teacher provides the service of educating students, and a police officer provides the service of keeping the community safe. Sometimes people provide a service that produces a good, such as a chef who prepares a meal. People pay money for goods and services. When you pay a producer of goods, she can use the money to purchase the materials to make more goods. When you pay a service provider, he can use the money to pay for more training so that he can do his job even better. Providers also use the money to pay for basic items such as food and shelter. When newscasters report that the economy is strong, it means that most people are happy with the amount of money, goods, and services they have.

14.   What is the main idea of this passage?

    a.   Newscasters often talk about the economy.

    b.   Sometimes the economy is strong, and other times it is weak.

    c.   The economy is a system in which goods and services are exchanged for money.

15.   What are goods?_____

16.   List two examples of goods. _____

17.   What are services? _____

18.   List two examples of service providers. _____

_____

**FACTOID:** Camels have three sets of eyelids to protect their eyes from sand.

PLACE STICKER HERE

**Complete the graph using the information in the table.**

| Day | Temperature (°F) |
|---|---|
| Monday | 87° |
| Tuesday | 90° |
| Wednesday | 74° |
| Thursday | 78° |
| Friday | 80° |

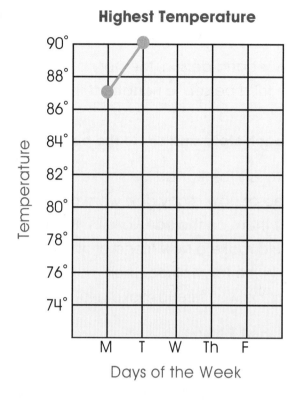

## Put on Your Dancing Shoes!

To boost your endurance, you have to push yourself so that your heart beats faster and you breathe harder. Dancing can be one of the most enjoyable ways to build your endurance, and it may not feel like exercise! Find an open area where you can move to your favorite upbeat tunes. Start by dancing continuously for 10 minutes several times per week. You do not need any dance training; simply move to the music's beat. Gradually increase the length of each dance time for an even better aerobic workout. Dancing is not only good for endurance, but it can also improve your mood, decrease anxiety, improve sleep, relieve stress, and raise self-esteem.

* See page ii.

# DAY 19

Point of view refers to the person who is telling the story or who is "speaking."

A story can be told from three different points of view:

- In first person, the main character tells the story.
- In second person, the story is told as though it is happening to you.
- In third person, a narrator tells the story as if she is watching it happen.

**Read each story and circle the point of view.**

1. Marcus's family had just moved to a large city from a very small town. He was surprised at how many cars were on the street and how few people said hello when he met them on the sidewalk. In his old town, he had known everyone. He hoped that he would make a new friend on the first day of school. When he saw the crowded hallways, he felt worried. Then, he thought to himself that with all of those people around, he was sure to make a lot of friends.

**First Person**          **Second Person**          **Third Person**

2. When my family moved to the big city, I was excited about all of the new activities we could try. I never thought how crowded it might be. Back home, my neighbors were friendly. It seemed like I knew everyone in the whole town. I wanted to make new friends in the city, but when I got to school, the hallways were so packed that I could hardly get to my classroom. I took a deep breath and said to myself, "With all of these people around, I am sure to make new friends!"

**First Person**          **Second Person**          **Third Person**

3. You and your family have just moved to the city. You are surprised to see so many cars on the road. In your old town, you felt like you knew everyone. When you drive up to the school, your mother wishes you good luck. You walk into the building and start to look for your classroom. You think to yourself that with all of these people around, you are sure to make some new friends.

**First Person**          **Second Person**          **Third Person**

**FITNESS FLASH:** Do 10 jumping jacks.

* See page ii.

PLACE STICKER HERE

**Circle the language arts words in the puzzle. Words can go across and down.**

| | | | | |
|---|---|---|---|---|
| body | alphabetical | adjectives | suffix | vowel |
| plural | consonant | nouns | pronoun | accent |
| syllable | prefix | verb | adverbs | singular |

```
i  a  l  p  h  a  b  e  t  i  c  a  l  g  c  p  l  u  r  a  l
u  d  m  n  a  j  k  n  a  c  c  e  n  t  o  h  q  b  k  e  y
o  j  v  o  w  e  l  o  c  s  i  y  s  m  n  u  s  v  x  d  o
j  e  m  u  p  r  e  f  i  x  u  p  y  b  s  i  u  e  m  p  n
f  c  q  n  r  i  m  b  t  c  o  e  l  n  o  w  f  j  r  h  e
b  t  k  s  o  u  g  u  o  d  c  x  l  k  n  n  f  t  q  w  a
a  i  v  s  n  d  r  i  x  i  i  z  a  j  a  b  i  v  e  r  b
p  v  b  i  o  s  b  a  d  v  e  r  b  s  n  x  x  o  x  f  k
r  e  l  s  u  i  s  d  c  u  u  p  l  d  t  m  o  h  j  i  c
y  s  j  i  n  x  q  w  m  y  d  s  e  p  b  g  p  i  u  n  l
k  m  t  u  d  s  i  n  g  u  l  a  r  h  v  k  b  o  d  y  g
o  t  j  q  e  w  a  z  x  s  w  e  d  c  v  f  r  t  g  b  n
```

# DAY 20

**Read the passage. Then, answer the questions.**

## City Services

Cities provide many services to the people who live there. The mayor and city council, who are elected by the citizens of a city, make the laws that everyone must follow. They also meet to discuss community issues, such as whether to build a new recreation center. Other city employees include police officers and firefighters. These people work to keep everyone in the city safe. Other city services include the library, where the public can check out books, and companies that provide water and electricity. Some cities have special programs for the people who live there, such as reading clubs at the library or computer classes for senior citizens. It takes many services to make a city work. Some people like to give back to their communities by doing volunteer work. They might teach swimming lessons or offer to pick up litter in the parks. When everyone in a city works together, it can be a great place to live.

1. What is the main idea of this passage?

    a. People living in a city receive many services.

    b. Some people like to give back to their communities.

    c. A library is a place where people can check out books.

2. Who elects the mayor and the city council? _____

    _____

3. What do the mayor and city council members do? _____

    _____

4. Name three employees who work for the city. _____

    _____

**CHARACTER CHECK:** Think of something that upsets you. How might you show tolerance toward it?

PLACE STICKER HERE

## Global Climates

Climate is the pattern of weather that occurs in a certain area over a long period of time. In this experiment, you will see why certain areas of the earth have different climates and temperatures.

**Materials:**
- adjustable gooseneck lamp
- 2 thermometers
- ruler
- globe
- duct tape
- timer or clock

**Procedure:**

1. Position the lamp about one foot (30 cm) from the globe. Because Earth is tilted on its axis (23.5°), position the globe so that the northern hemisphere is tilted away from the lamp. In this position, the northern hemisphere is experiencing winter.

2. On the side of the globe nearest the lamp, use two small pieces of duct tape to attach one thermometer over the equator and the other thermometer near the north pole.

3. Record the initial temperature at each location in the table below.

4. Turn on the lamp. Record the temperatures again after five minutes.

| Reading | North Pole | Equator |
|---|---|---|
| Initial temperature (°F) | | |
| Temperature after five minutes (°F) | | |

**Conclusions:**
**Answer the questions on a separate sheet of paper.**

1. Was there a difference between the initial and final temperatures? Why?

2. What was the difference in the final temperature between the north pole and the equator? Give an explanation for your results.

3. What if you positioned the globe so that the northern hemisphere was tilted toward the lamp? Predict how the temperature at the north pole might be different. Then, conduct an experiment to test your prediction.

4. How does this explain the process that causes different climates on Earth?

## BONUS

### Solar and Lunar Eclipses

An eclipse can occur when the light of the sun becomes blocked by the moon or Earth. Two types of shadows can be observed during an eclipse: an umbra and a penumbra. The umbra is the darkest part of a shadow. If you are standing in the umbra, the source of light is completely blocked by the object causing the shadow. This is different from the penumbra, in which the light source is only partially blocked, and there is only a partial shadow.

**Procedure:**

1.  Use a ruler to draw two straight lines from point **A** on the sun through points **C** and **D** on the moon. Stop the lines when they strike the edge of Earth.

2.  Draw two additional straight lines from point **B** on the sun through points **C** and **D** on the moon. Stop the lines when they strike the edge of Earth.

3.  Use a colorful pencil to shade in the **umbra**. Using a different color, shade in the **penumbra**. Show what colors you used in the key.

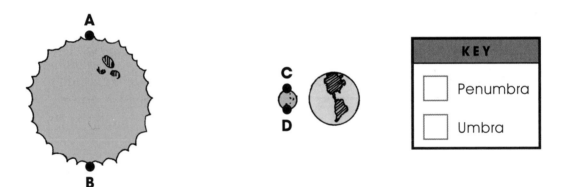

**Conclusions:**

**Answer the questions on a separate sheet of paper.**

1.  Name the type of eclipse pictured in the diagram.

2.  During which phase of the moon would this type of eclipse occur?

3.  If you were observing this eclipse from Earth, in which part of the shadow would you need to be to observe a total eclipse?

4.  With an adult, use the Internet to find out when you may be able to view this type of eclipse.

## Chile

**Use the graph to answer the questions.**

### Main Economic Sectors in Chile

11%

55%

34%

■ Agriculture

□ Industry

▨ Services

1.  The total of the agricultural and industrial sectors equals _____.

    a.  89%                          b.  11%

    c.  34%                          d.  45%

2.  More than half of the economy is supported by the _____ sector.

    a.  agriculture                  b.  industry

    c.  services                     d.  mining

3.  The services sector produces _____ times as much as the agriculture sector.

    a.  two                          b.  four

    c.  five                         d.  ten

4.  The smallest sector of the economy is the _____ sector.

    a.  agriculture                  b.  industry

    c.  services                     d.  mining

## BONUS

### Deforestation

Deforestation is the cutting down, burning, and damaging of forests. In Brazil, this refers to the tropical rain forest called the Amazon. Forests are cut for agricultural purposes, such as planting crops or grazing cattle, as well as for commercial logging. The problems resulting from deforestation include an increase in global warming and the extinction of many species of plants and animals. The government of Brazil has used several programs to preserve the remaining rain forests, but many people are still concerned over the continued destruction of the Amazon rain forest.

**Use the chart to answer the questions.**

| Rate of Deforestation in Brazil | |
| --- | --- |
| Years | Square Kilometers (Miles) |
| 1989–1990 | 13,810 (8,581) |
| 1990–1991 | 11,130 (6,916) |
| 1991–1992 | 13,786 (8,566) |
| 1992–1994 | 14,896 (9,256) |
| 1994–1995 | 29,059 (18,056) |
| 1995–1996 | 18,161 (11,285) |
| 1996–1997 | 13,227 (8,219) |
| 1997–1998 | 17,383 (10,801) |

1.  The smallest amount of deforestation took place between _____.

    a.  1996–1997      b.  1989–1990      c.  1994–1995      d.  1990–1991

2.  More deforestation took place between 1992 and 1994 than between _____.

    a.  1995–1996      b.  1991–1992      c.  1994–1995      d.  1997–1998

3.  Between 1989 and 1991, what was the decrease in square kilometers of deforestation?

    a.  4,680      b.  2,680      c.  24,940      d.  4,933

# South American Time Line

**Use the time line to answer the questions.**

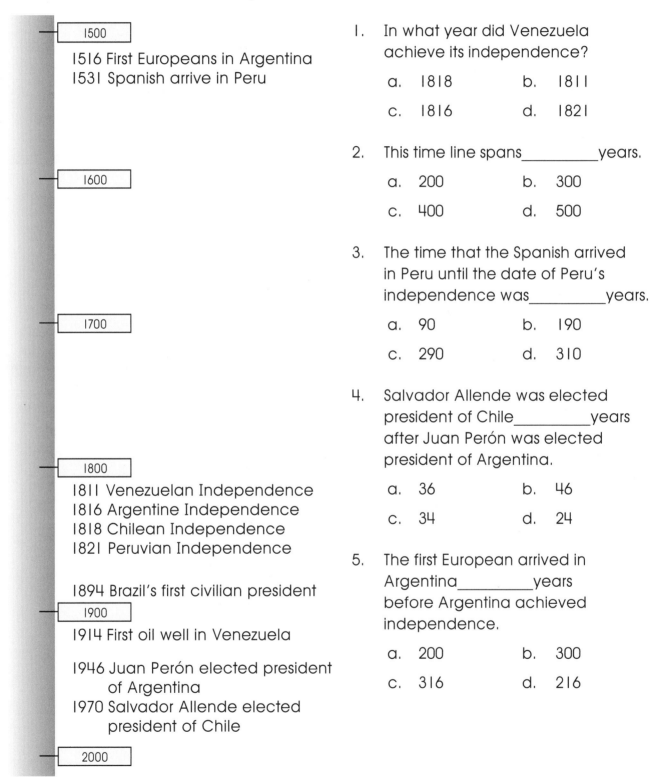

1500

1516 First Europeans in Argentina
1531 Spanish arrive in Peru

1600

1700

1800

1811 Venezuelan Independence
1816 Argentine Independence
1818 Chilean Independence
1821 Peruvian Independence

1894 Brazil's first civilian president

1900

1914 First oil well in Venezuela

1946 Juan Perón elected president
     of Argentina
1970 Salvador Allende elected
     president of Chile

2000

1. In what year did Venezuela achieve its independence?

   a. 1818          b. 1811

   c. 1816          d. 1821

2. This time line spans_____years.

   a. 200           b. 300

   c. 400           d. 500

3. The time that the Spanish arrived in Peru until the date of Peru's independence was_____years.

   a. 90            b. 190

   c. 290           d. 310

4. Salvador Allende was elected president of Chile_____years after Juan Perón was elected president of Argentina.

   a. 36            b. 46

   c. 34            d. 24

5. The first European arrived in Argentina_____years before Argentina achieved independence.

   a. 200           b. 300

   c. 316           d. 216

# BONUS

## Take It Outside!

Invite a friend or family member to join you outside for a picnic. Pack foods that must be divided into pieces or sections, like oranges, sandwiches, and pizza. When you arrive at your eating spot, explain that this is a percentage picnic. As you share each item, cut out the portions and point out the percentages of items that you are eating. For example, you may give your friend 25 percent of an orange, but he might only eat 50 percent of the portion.

During the summer, nature provides wonderful inspiration for art. Seek and capture an outdoor image or scene that you find extraordinary. For example, you may find the combination of colors the moment before the sun sets to be inspiring. Use a variety of art materials, such as torn paper, fabric swatches, wallpaper scraps, glue, markers, and foam board, to design a three-dimensional piece of artwork that shows the qualities of the scene.

The characteristics of many plants and animals are inherited. However, the characteristics of some plants and animals change as a result of their environments. These changes are called adaptations. With an adult, go online or visit the library to learn more about the plants and animals that live near you. Then, go on a nature walk. Look for plants and animals that you read about, such as birds, insects, and flowers, and observe them. As you observe them, think about how each plant or animal adapted to survive in its environment.

* See page ii.

**Section I**

**Day 1:** 1. 8; 2. 6; 3. 12; 4. 11; 5. 5; 6. 10; 7. 30; 8. 5; 9. 18; 10. 8; 11. 18; 12. 9; 13. 3; 14. 9; 15. 13; 16. 6; 17. 7; 18. 8; 19. 7; 20. 24; 21. 0; 22. yes; 23. yes; 24. yes; 25. no; 26. no; 27. yes; 28. yes; 29. yes; 30. no; 31. no; 32. no; 33. no; 34. enemy; 35. time; 36. overlook; 37. sky

**Day 2:** 1. $7 + 9 = 16$, $16 - 9 = 7$, $16 - 7 = 9$; 2. $9 \times 3 = 27$, $27 \div 9 = 3$, $27 \div 3 = 9$; 3. $5 \times 8 = 40$, $40 \div 8 = 5$, $40 \div 5 = 8$; 4. $8 + 3 = 11$, $11 - 8 = 3$, $11 - 3 = 8$; 5. $4 \times 3 = 12$, $12 \div 4 = 3$, $12 \div 3 = 4$; 6. $7 + 2 = 9$, $9 - 2 = 7$, $9 - 7 = 2$; 7. Sunday–Sun.; 8. quart–qt.; 9. ounce–oz.; 10. example–ex.; 11. Friday–Fri.; 12. pound–lb.; 13. pint–pt.; 14. October–Oct.; 15. 500 years; 16. 274 feet (83.5 m); 17. The weather turned colder and people trample the ground near the trees' roots; 18. warmth and water

**Day 3:** 1. $90 - 10 = 80$; 2. $100 - 10 = 90$; 3. $90 - 40 = 50$; 4. $900 - 600 = 300$; 5. $60 - 40 = 20$; 6. $20 + 40 = 60$; 7. $200 + 200 = 400$; 8. $60 + 40 = 100$; 9. Christopher Columbus, **explorer**; 10. Antarctica, **continent**; 11. **We, canoe**, Red River; 12. Fido, **dog**; 13. San Francisco, **city, bay**; 14. **She, aunt**, Boston; 15. Mt. Mitchell, **mountain**; 16. Thursday, **birthday**; A. 3:00; B. 9:00; C. 3:30; 17. 3:50 P.M.; 18. 3:00 A.M.; 19. 8:35 A.M.; 20. 3:00 A.M.; 21. 5:05 A.M.; 22. 5 hours, 30 minutes; 23. Answers will vary but may include sap, map, jam, am, as; 24. Answers will vary but may include worm, to, mow, tow, row, or, rot; 25. Answers will vary but may include man, form, pen, from, can, romance, farm, more

**Day 4:** Patterns will vary; Mr. Greg Jones, 1461 Condor St., Lake Tona, OH 98562; 1. b; 2. the study of stars, planets, and the universe; 3. to see stars and to measure their distance from Earth and their speed; 4. when certain objects will appear in the sky; 5. It was named after Edmund Halley, the person who accurately predicted its return.

**Day 5:** 1. The following words should be underlined: boy, coach, friend, sister, teacher, doctor, assistant, student, actor; 2. The following words should be underlined: laboratory, park, clinic, playground, classroom, office, hallway, diner; 3. The following words should be underlined: desk, truck, window, dictionary, banana, book, house, lunch box, ruler; 4.–5. Answers will vary; 6. 826; 7. 309; 8. 8,846; 9. 296; 10. 322; 11. 3,991; 12. 132; 13. 362; 14. there; 15. their; 16. their; 17. there; 18. there; 19.–20. Answers will vary.

**Day 6:** 1. smallest; 2. loudest; 3. shortest; 4. fastest; 5. happiest; 6. biggest; 7.–11. Answers will vary.

**Day 7:** 1. 9; 2. 0; 3. -8; 4. 4; 5. -2; 6. <; 7. >; 8. >; 9. <; 10. >; 11. >; Answers will vary; 12. a.; 13. Answers may include lizards, snakes, turtles, crocodiles; 14. frogs, toads, salamanders; 15. cold-blooded, egg-laying

**Day 8:** 1. 5; 2. 7; 3. 2; 4. 0; 5. 7; 6. 6; 7. 8; 8. 5; 9. 9; 10. 7; 11. 3; 12. 9; 13. 8; 14. 4; 15. 8; 16. 9; 17. 8; 18. 4; 19. 5; 20. 6; 21. 6; 22. **had**, <u>finished</u>; 23. **have**, <u>enjoyed</u>; 24. **were**, <u>cleaning</u>; 25. **have been**, <u>sleeping</u>; Answers will vary, but may include: 26. was; 27. was; 28. am; 29. were; 30. pre; 31. dis; 32. re; 33. tri; 34. uni; 35. re; 36. un; 37. bi; 38. This metaphor means that your smile is cheerful; 39. This metaphor means that winning the award was amazing; 40. This metaphor means that the store is confusing to walk through; 41. This metaphor means that the pillow was soft.

**Day 9:** 1. 2 nickels, 1 penny; 2. 1 dime, 1 nickel, 5 pennies; 3. 1 quarter, 1 dime, 2 nickels, 2 pennies; 4. 1 quarter, 2 nickels, 1 dime; 5. 3 nickels, 2 pennies; 6. 2 dimes, 4 nickels; 7. bunnies; 8. movies; 9. window; 10. branches; 11. city; 12. geese; 13. children; 14. feet; 15. toes; 16. box; 17. library; 18. man; 19. bus; 20. classes; 21. c; 22. Africa, Asia, Australia, Antarctica, Europe, North America, South America; 23. a; 24. about 6 times or 14 million $mi^2$ (36.3 million $km^2$)

**Day 10:** They, they, It, it, He, us, They, it, He, It, them; 1. 18; 2. 9; 3. 63; 4. 32; 5. 28; 6. 81; 7. 30; 8. 24; 9. 40; 10. 21; 11. 9;

12. 12; 13. 24; 14. 18; 15. 25; 16. 45; 17. 54; 18. 56; 19. 64; 20. 27; 21. 49; Answers and drawings will vary; 22. hides; 23. dashes; 24. searches; 25. sits; 26. kneels; 27. crawls; 28. races; 29. finds

**Day 11:** 1.–6. Parallel lines should be drawn; 7.–16. Answers will vary; 17. bridge; 18. country; 19. city; 20. person; 21. ocean; 22. bell; 23. month; 24. person; 25. 7; 26. 8; 27. 7; 28. 5; 29. 9; 30. 5; 31. 4; 32. 5. 33. 8; 34. 4; 35. 2; 36. 9; 37. 1; 38. 4; 39. 7; 40. 7; 41. 5; 42. 8; 43. 9; 44. 3; 45. knew; 46. wrote; 47. brought; 48. began; 49. grew

**Day 12:** 1. 3,983; 2. 11,701; 3. 30,388; 4. 31,731; 5. 21,701; 6. 12,293; 7. 8,667; 8. 10,354; 9. sun's; 10. child's; 11. shirt's; 12. dog's; 13. cows'; 14. birds'; 15. >; 16. =; 17. <; 18. <; 19. >; 20. =; 21. >; 22. >; 23. <; 24. <; 25. >; 26. >; 27. <; 28. <; Because they are smart "kids"!

**Day 13:** Stories will vary; 1. a; 2. popular government, or government by the people; 3. People vote on every decision; 4. People elect leaders who represent their viewpoints and vote on the issues.

**Day 14:** 1. isn't; 2. they'll; 3. should've; 4. you're; 5. we'd; 6.–9. Answers will vary, but may include:

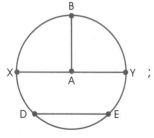

10.–14. Answers will vary; 15. wrote; 16. taught; 17. drew; 18. found; 19. spoke; 20. felt; 21. held; 22. bent; 23. heard; 24. caught; 25. saw; 26. made; 27. stuck

**Day 15:** 1. 1,782; 2. 3,777; 3. 1,786; 4. 5,408; 5. 1,089; 6. 4,593; 7. 33,802; 8. 53,668; 9. key's/keys'; 10. bird's/birds'; 11. mouse's/mice's; 12. puppy's/puppies'; 13. woman's/women's; 14. class's/classes'

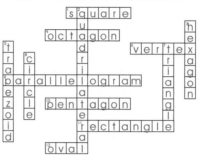

**Day 16:** 1. went; 2. are; 3. hid; 4. rode; 5. digging; 6.–10. Answers will vary; 11. 3,786; 12. 10,725; 13. 2,976; 14. 29,291; 15. 92,685; 16. 15,255; 17. 22,316; 18. 15,011; 19. thank; 20. hopped; 21. call; 22. skated; 23. sprain; 24. loved; 25. wrap; 26. played; 27. hug

**Day 17:** 1.–6. Answers will vary; 7. aboard, about, above, affect, afford; 8. after, aggravate, agree, aid, ailment; 9. c; 10. The mayor works with the city council to plan activities and solutions to the city's problems; 11. different parts of the city; 12. makes sure that city services are running smoothly and creates a budget; 13. a.

**Day 18:** 1. 16; 2. 45; 3. 16; 4. 10; 5. 32; 6. 42; 7. 0; 8. 18; 9. 27; 10. 20; 11. 40; 12. 36; 13. 6; 14. 0;

15. 0; 16. 15; 17. 24; 18. 12; 19. 24; 20. 64; 21.–28. Answers will vary; Stories will vary.

**Day 19:** 1. to stay healthy; 2. whether you are a girl or boy, how active you are, and your age; 3.–4. Answers will vary; 5. Emmett, Hugo, Boy Scouts; 6. Idaho, Rashad, Snake River; 7. Sierra, Winn Elementary School; 8. Doug, Brookstown Mall; 9. Ms. Hernandez's, Lincoln Memorial, Washington, D.C.; 10. Niagara Falls, Canada; 11. $2.27; 12. $20.40; 13. $45; 14. $2.75; 15. now in progress; 16. information, awareness, understanding; 17. doubt; 18. leaving no room for error, accurate; 19. a kind of light; 20. occupation, source of livelihood; 21. worldwide, understood by all; 22. the science and art of farming; 23. to make clearly known

**Day 20:** 1. admire; 2. pedal; 3. glisten; 4. doubt; 5. pause; 6. comfort; Drawings will vary; 7.-12. Answers will vary.

**Page 46:** 1. 55, 11; 2. 50, 10; 3. 20, 4; 4. 40, 8; 5. 30, 6; 6. 20, 4; 7. 90, 18; 8. 50, 10

**Page 47:** 1. 1:00 P.M.; 2. 1:00 P.M.; 3. 10:00 A.M.; 4. 4:00 P.M.; 5. 10:00 A.M.

**Secton II**

**Day 1:** Answers will vary.

**Day 2:** 1. 72; 2. 48; 3. 132; 4. 36; 5. 92; 6. 161; 7. 204; 8. 80; 9. 390; 10. 602; 11. 621; 12. 228; 13. 372; 14. 679; 15. 166; 16.–19. Answers will vary; 20. 2, 3, 4, 5, 6; 21. 3, 40, 4, 50, 5, 60, 6; 22. 2, 18, 4, 30, 6; 23.–27. Answers will vary.

**Day 3:** 1.–5. Answers will vary; 6. you, us; 7. us; 8. we; 9. We, them; 10. He; 11. You; 12. him; 13. It, her; 14. She, me; 15. He, I; 16. pat, tap; 17. ten, net; 18. gab, bag; 19. loop, pool; 20. now, won; 21. pins, snip

**Day 4:** 1.–4. Answers will vary; 5. a; 6. They make sure that everyone follows the laws of the community to keep people safe; 7. They put out fires and educate people about fire safety; 8. They pick up everybody's trash; 9. They make sure that city parks are clean and safe so that people can play or have picnics in them.

**Day 5:** 1. 40; 2. 3,600; 3. 5,600; 4. 240; 5. 100; 6. 4,000; 7. 720; 8. 300; 9. 3,000; 10. 400; 11. 560; 12. 3,500; 13. 6,300; 14. 2,400; 15. 3,600; 16. 7,200; 17. 1,600; 18. 6,300; 19. 30; 20. 4,200; 21. 2,400; 22. 280; 23. 90; 24. 1,000; 25. We; 26. It; 27. They; 28. He; 29. birch; 30. three; 31. holly; 32. birch; 33. brown, creamy white, dark gray, ash; 34. maple; 35. Answers will vary.

**Day 6:**

| × | 10 | 20 | 30 | 40 | 50 | 60 | 70 | 80 | 90 |
|---|----|----|----|----|----|----|----|----|----|
| 1 | 10 | 20 | 30 | 40 | 50 | 60 | 70 | 80 | 90 |
| 2 | 20 | 40 | 60 | 80 | 100 | 120 | 140 | 160 | 180 |
| 3 | 30 | 60 | 90 | 120 | 150 | 180 | 210 | 240 | 270 |
| 4 | 40 | 80 | 120 | 160 | 200 | 240 | 280 | 320 | 360 |
| 5 | 50 | 100 | 150 | 200 | 250 | 300 | 350 | 400 | 450 |
| 6 | 60 | 120 | 180 | 240 | 300 | 360 | 420 | 480 | 540 |
| 7 | 70 | 140 | 210 | 280 | 350 | 420 | 490 | 560 | 630 |
| 8 | 80 | 160 | 240 | 320 | 400 | 480 | 560 | 640 | 720 |
| 9 | 90 | 180 | 270 | 360 | 450 | 540 | 630 | 720 | 810 |

Multiplying by hundreds has one more zero; by adding a zero to each number; 1. you're; 2. your; 3. it's; 4. Its; 5. your; 6. Its; 7. b; 8. c; 9. People gather for a special meal and a reading of Burns's poetry.

**Day 7:** Jan., GA, NY, Mon., Mar., Wed., Apr., gal., in., yd, g, adv., adj., mph, Ave., D.C.; 1. 5; 2. 2; 3. 1; 4. 4; 5. 3; 6. She is not telling the truth; 7. Do you think we'll be in trouble?; 8. You do not notice time passing when you are busy doing something you enjoy; 9. Shanice got right to the point; 10. He will help out; 11. Bob will run around the block; 12. I will have corn tomorrow; 13. Troy will catch the ball; 14. He may go to the new school; 15. Davion will wash the dog.

**Day 8:** 1. years; 2. days; 3. months; 4. hours; 5. minutes; 6. minutes; 7. weeks; 8. evening, events, eventually, every; 9. treasure, treatment, tree, tremendous; 10. coal, coast, coconut, collect; 11. end, enthusiasm, entrance, entry; 12. 3, 30, 300; 13. 4, 40, 400; 14. 3, 30, 300; 15. 2, 20, 200; 16. 5, 50, 500; 17. 9, 90, 900; 18. 4, 40, 400; 19. 7, 70, 700; 20. noun; 21. verb; 22. noun; 23. verb; 24. verb; 25. verb

**Day 9:** 1. 31 R2; 2. 11 R3; 3. 21 R1; 4. 11 R3; 5. 32 R1; 6. 11 R1; 7. 11 R2; 8. 11 R2; 9. har/ness; 10. live/li/ness; 11. in/flate; 12. ca/ble; 13. glo/ri/ous; 14. wash/ing; 15. pi/geon; 16. ap/ple; 17. jew/el/ry; 18. ma/ple; 19. bi/cy/cle; 20. fro/zen; 21. dif/fi/cult; 22. ten/nis; 23. hap/py

**Day 10:** 1.–7. Answers will vary; 8. b; 9. They are easy to walk on; 10. a; 11. They were too difficult to navigate.

**Day 11:** 1. $\frac{1}{4}$; 2. $\frac{2}{6}$ or $\frac{1}{3}$; 3. $\frac{1}{2}$; 4. $\frac{3}{5}$; 5. $\frac{2}{4}$ or $\frac{1}{2}$; 6. $\frac{4}{12}$ or $\frac{1}{3}$; 7. $\frac{3}{4}$; 8. $\frac{1}{3}$; 9. soil; 10. right; 11. obtuse; 12. acute; 13. obtuse; 14. acute; 15. right

**Day 12:** 1. >; 2. >; 3. >; 4. =; 5. >; 6. <; 7. >; 8. >; 9. <; 10. =; 11. =; 12. <; 13. Lin, Paco, Julie, and Keesha are going to a movie; 14. Anna took her spelling, reading, and math books to school; 15. The snack bar is only open Monday, Tuesday, Friday, and Saturday; 16. Our new school flag is blue, green, yellow, black, and orange; 17. Many women, men, children, and pets enjoy sledding; 18. Have you seen the kittens, chicks, or goslings; 19. a; 20. put seed in a bird feeder or hang a birdhouse; 21. Answers will vary but may include: What birds like to eat or how they develop over time; 22. binoculars

**Day 13:** 1. 810; 2. 796; 3. 7,232; 4. 1,645; 5. 1,680; 6. 2,592; 7. 3,296; 8. 4,878; math words: measure, numerator, estimate, equal to, hexagon, (intersection); geography words: region, hemisphere, basin, elevation, equator; transportation words: interstate, speed, highway, yield, intersection; science words: environment, larva, insect, bacteria, recycle, (colony); social studies: debate, freedom, society, colony, candidate; 9. magazine; 10. serious; 11. represent; 12. thought; 13. remember; 14. unbroken; 15. factory; 16. difficult; 17. industry; 18. whistle

**Day 14:** 1.–5. Answers will vary; 6. Yes, I will go with you,

Tristan; 7. Wynona, I am glad Zoe will come; 8. Aaron, do you play tennis; 9. Yes, I went to the doctor's office; 10. Raul, do you want to go; 11. Neyla, what happened; 12. No, I never learned how to fish; 13. Mom, thanks for the help; 14. No, I need to finish this; 15. Hugo, I found a penny; 16. Come on, T.J., let's go to the game; 17. Tell me, Crystal, did you do this?

**Day 15:**

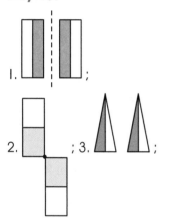

4. "Nate, do you have the map of our town?" asked Kit.; 5. "What an exciting day I had!" cried Janelle.; 6. I said, "The puppy chewed up my sneaker."; 7. "Did you know that birds' bones are hollow?" asked Mrs. Tyler.; 8. She answered, "No, I did not know that."; 9. Wayne exclaimed, "I won first prize in the pie-baking contest!"; 10. "I'm tired after raking the yard," said Sadie.; 11. "I am too," replied Sarah.; 12. a; 13. the instruments they use and the results they find; 14. Everyone learns more about the subjects; 15. to make sure that you are being safe

**Day 16:** 1. St. Patrick's Day; 2. Valentine's Day; 3. Independence Day; 4. Halloween; 5. Labor Day; 6. January; 7. Father's Day; 8. braid; 9. list; 10. moon; 11. world; 12. gondola; 13. spray; 14. flash; 15. certain; 16. genuine, great; 17. terrible, straight; 18. among, awhile; 19. where, weather; 20. junior, journey; 21. remain, refer; 22. feathers, fiction; 23. drawer, detective; 24. holiday, healthy; 25. explore, enormous; 26. I; 27. They; 28. me; 29. We; 30. him; 31. I; 32. her

**Day 17:** 1. 2; 2. 8; 3. 6; 4. 2; 5. 2; 6. 10; 7. 6; 8. 3; 9. 8; 10. 0; 11. 3; 12. 5; 13. 2; 14. 1; 15. 10; 16. 8; 17. artificial; 18. schedule; 19. exchange; 20. reputation; 21. assistant; 22. genuine; 23. campaign; 24. publicize; 25. b; 26. when Earth moves between the sun and moon and blocks some sunlight from reaching the moon; 27. It is dark from Earth's shadow; 28. when the moon moves between the sun and Earth and blocks some sunlight from reaching Earth

**Day 18:** circle: a, c, d, e; 1. They are polygons because they have straight lines and are closed figures; 2. 3 sides, 3 vertices; 3. 5 sides, 5 vertices; 4. 4 sides, 4 vertices; 5. 8 sides, 8 vertices; 6. Millions of Cats; 7. Higher Than the Arrow; 8. John Paul Jones; 9. No Flying in the House; 10. Ludo and the Star Horse; 11. An Elephant Is Not a Cat; 12. One Wide River to Cross; 13. The Tropic Express; 14.–16. Answers will vary.

**Day 19:** 1. Dr.; 2. Rd.; 3. Ms.; 4. Mon., TX; 5. Mr.; 6. Ave.; 7. tbsp.; 8. Tues.; 9. Jan.; 10. Mr.; 11. St.; 12. tsp.; 13. Thurs.

**Day 20:** 1. $3\frac{2}{3}$; 2. $1\frac{1}{8}$; 3. $2\frac{2}{3}$; 4. $2\frac{1}{2}$; 5. $1\frac{3}{4}$; 6. $3\frac{1}{3}$; 7. $1\frac{1}{10}$; 8. $1\frac{3}{7}$; 9. $2\frac{3}{8}$; 10. $2\frac{1}{2}$; 11. $1\frac{4}{5}$; 12. $3\frac{1}{10}$; 13. $2\frac{3}{10}$; 14. $2\frac{1}{8}$; 15. $4\frac{1}{3}$; 16. a; 17. c; 18. b; 19. a; 20. d

**Page 93:** 1. a; 2. a; 3. b; 4. a

**Page 94:** 1. b; 2. Alice Springs; 3. Melbourne; 4. Great Barrier Reef; 5. Perth

**Page 95:** 1. d; 2. c; 3. a; 4. b

**Section III**

**Day 1:** 1. $\frac{14}{10}$ or $1\frac{2}{5}$; 2. $\frac{8}{4}$ or 2; 3. $\frac{11}{11}$ or 1; 4. $\frac{24}{12}$ or 2; 5. $\frac{13}{11}$ or $1\frac{2}{11}$; 6. $\frac{15}{12}$ or $1\frac{1}{4}$; 7. $\frac{11}{8}$ or 1; 8. $\frac{15}{15}$ or 1; 9. $\frac{18}{16}$ or $1\frac{1}{8}$; 10. $\frac{9}{7}$ or $1\frac{2}{7}$; 11. $\frac{14}{9}$ or $1\frac{5}{9}$; 12. a; 13. Greenwich, England; 14. people who study geography and mapmaking and explorers around the world; 15. Answers will vary.

**Day 2:**

| v | o | l | t | a | g | e | a | i | t | q | w | t | n |
| b | r | e | s | i | s | t | a | n | c | e | i | l | k |
| a | h | u | t | w | a | t | t | s | g | y | r | z | b |
| t | e | c | g | j | m | d | x | u | q | k | e | e | v |
| t | y | o | f | h | v | k | u | l | z | b | s | r | h |
| e | f | n | r | o | w | g | d | a | a | q | a | z | x |
| r | j | d | h | n | b | v | f | t | r | e | w | n | s |
| u | j | u | y | u | i | j | m | o | k | i | o | e | p |
| z | i | c | q | w | c | u | r | r | e | n | t | g | l |
| p | g | t | a | m | z | x | s | e | d | c | v | a | m |
| c | l | o | s | e | d | c | i | r | c | u | i | t | j |
| b | g | r | t | t | y | h | n | m | j | u | o | i | u |
| o | l | p | m | a | q | p | o | s | i | t | i | v | e |
| h | y | u | j | l | w | r | y | i | p | k | h | e | f |

1. $\frac{1}{6}$; 2. $\frac{2}{10}$ or $\frac{1}{5}$; 3. $\frac{1}{4}$; 4. $3\frac{4}{10}$ or $3\frac{2}{5}$; 5. $5\frac{1}{10}$; 6. $4\frac{1}{15}$

July 17, 2015

Dear David,

Thank you for sending me the pictures from your trip. It looks like you had a great time! Do you want me to send them back?

Next week, I'm going to Kansas City with my dad. I can't wait!

Your friend,
Greg

**Day 3:** 1. 2,994; 2. 4,249; 3. 4,677; 4. 11,035; 5. 12,979; 6. 3,304; 7. 10,165; 8. 5,785; 9. 2,085; 10. 11,155; 11. 10,020; 12. 2,073; 13. b; 14. groups of people who feel the same way about one or more issues; 15. Answers will vary; 16. rose, oak tree, dove

**Day 4:** 1. 10; 2. 80; 3. 10,000; 4. 144; 5. 2; 6. 14,000; 7. 4; 8. 176; 9. 6,000; 10. 20,000; 11. 2; 12. 48; 13. cells; 14. water; 15. iron, calcium; 16. digestive; 17. circulatory; 18.–23. Answers will vary, but may include: 18. bumpy, smooth; 19. trouble, solution; 20. fascinating, boring; 21. shock, expectation; 22. cheerful, sad; 23. collect, plant

**Day 5:** 1. quietquippers.joke; 2. ruhilarious.joke; 3. 36,959 visitors; 4. 12,455 visitors; 5. 9,129 visitors; 6. 61,593 visitors; 7. c; 8. the outlines of the continents and seas; 9. important buildings and streets; 10. north, south, east, and west

**Day 6:** 1. into; 2. depend; 3. bacon; 4. dial; 5. begin; 6. salad; 7. unlock; 8. table; 9. violin; 10. accept; 11. busy; 12. b; 13. pelican, alligator; 14. a pattern of stars; 15. Washington

**Day 7:** 1. $\frac{3}{10}$ or 0.3; 2. $\frac{9}{10}$ or 0.9; 3. $\frac{7}{10}$ or 0.7; 4. $\frac{1}{10}$ or 0.10; 5. $\frac{5}{10}$ or 0.5; 6. 0.3; 7. 1.7; 8. 3.5; 9. $1\frac{9}{10}$; 10. $\frac{8}{10}$; 11. $3\frac{4}{10}$; 12. will cook; 13. will visit; 14. will go; 15. will read; 16. will show; 17. will play; 18. girl; 19. king; 20. eat; 21. tree; 22. pilot; 23. jar; 24. break

**Day 8:** 1. 0.25; 2. 0.20; 3. 0.86; 4. 0.37; 5. 0.09; 6. 1.93; 7. 7.15; 8. 15.47; 9. 46.89; 10. 35.06; 11. 625.12; 12. tall/mountain, blue, yellow/flowers; 13. stronger/he; 14. fun, exciting/sledding; 15.–20. Answers will vary.

**Day 9:** 1. Olivia; 2. Isabella; 3. $25; 4. $30; 5. Lonny and Ava; 6. $72.50; 7. unhappy; 8. preheat; 9. bicycle; 10. review; 11. misunderstand; 12. unknown; 13. uncover; 14. uniform; 15. replace; 16. $159.92; 17. $44.22; 18. $142.50; 19. $3.23; 20. $348.81; 21. $7.11; 22. $1,005.12; 23. $57.42; 24.–32. Answers will vary.

**Day 10:** 1. Nutrients; 2. Exercise; 3. water; 4. food groups; 5. energy; 6. healthy; 7.–16. Answers will vary; 17. 700 (2 zeros); 18. 390 (1 zero); 19. 9,000 (3 zeros); 20. 36,000 (3 zeros); 21. 6,000 (3 zeros); 22. 4,600 (2 zeros); 23. 56,000 (3 zeros); 24. 250,000 (4 zeros); 25. 54,000 (3 zeros); 26. 132,000 (3 zeros); 27. 420,000 (4 zeros); 28. redder, reddest; 29. hotter, hottest; 30. nicer, nicest

**Day 11:** 1. 1,369,000; 2. 502,100,007; 3. three hundred seventy-five million four hundred three thousand one hundred one; 4. eight hundred ninety-four million three hundred thirty-six thousand forty-five; Answers will vary, but may include: My friend and I visited Cardiff, Wales. We learned that Cardiff is the capital and largest port of Wales. The city lies on the River Taff near the Bristol Channel. Cardiff is near the largest coal mines in Great Britian.; 5. b; 6. It gathers water and minerals; 7. sunlight, air, water, and minerals; 8. They help attract bees and butterflies, which bring pollen.

**Day 12:** 1. 2,691; 2. 1,296; 3. 3,060; 4. 2,001; 5. 3,542; 6. 2,793; 7. 2,993; 8. 4,560; 9. 5,808; 10. 6,256; 11. S; 12. A; 13. S; 14. S; 15. A; 16. S; 17. A; 18. H; 19. A; 20. H; 21. S; 22. A; 23. H; 24. S; 25. A; 26. S; 27. H; 28. H

**Day 13:** 8. a; 9. San Diego has a very mild climate, and New Orleans is humid; 10. Climate describes the weather in an area over a long period of time; 11. Climates near the equator are warmer than those at the poles.

**Day 14:** 1. 6 R9; 2. 6 R36; 3. 6 R24; 4. 9 R11; 5. 4 R6; 6. 5 R8; 7. 9 R33; 8. 4 R12; 9. 5 R10; 10. 11 R32; 11. 9 R31; 12. a; 13. They are fuels made from things like vegetable oil and are used like fossil fuels; 14. c.

**Day 15:** 1. isosceles; 2. scalene; 3. equilateral; 4. isosceles; 5. isosceles; 6. equilateral; 7. isosceles; 8. scalene; 9.–15. Answers will vary; 16. a; 17. obey the laws of their country, respect the opinions of others, help others in their community; 18. 18 years old; 19. right to a fair trial, right to speak freely, and right to practice any religion

**Day 16:** 1. $15.60; 2. $18.72; 3. $12.22; 4. $11.25; 5. $27.54; 6. $31.86; 7. $119.68; 8. $193.20; 9. 12 cm; 10. 15 cm; 11. 11.5 cm; 12. 8.5 cm; 13. the part of a line between two points; 14. lines that cross; 15. lines that do not cross; 16. the length of the sides of a closed figure; 17. when; 18. when; 19. how; 20. where; 21. how; 22. where

**Day 17:** 1. b; 2. a; 3. c; 4. b; 5. figures that are the same shape and size as each other; 6. a 90° angle; 7. a polygon with three straight sides; 8. a polygon with two pairs of parallel sides that are opposite of each other; 9. 2 cups; 10. 60 gal.; 11. 2 gal.; 12. 10; 13. 2; 14. 4; 15. 2; 16. 12; 17. 4

**Day 18:** 1.–6. Answers will vary; 7. The book was ripped **because** the dog chewed it; 8. **Because** it was so cold, Betty could ice-skate only for a short while; 9. I went to bed early last night **because** I was so tired; 10. **Because** it was raining hard, we couldn't play outside; 11. The rabbit ran away quickly **because** it saw a cat; 12. It was very foggy outside, **so** we could not see the mountains; 13. **Because**

we got to camp too late, there was no time for hiking; 14. c; 15. items that are produced; 16. books and clothing; 17. activities that people do for one another; 18. teacher and police officer

**Day 19:**

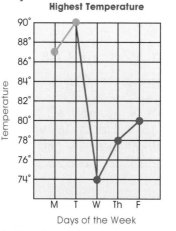

1. Third Person; 2. First Person; 3. Second Person

**Day 20:**

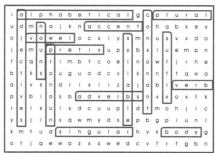

1. a; 2. the citizens of that city; 3. make the laws that everyone must follow; 4. police officers, firefighters, mayor

**Page 140:** 1. solar; 2. new moon; 3. umbra

**Page 141:** 1. d; 2. c; 3. c; 4. a

**Page 142:** 1. d; 2. b; 3. b

**Page 143:** 1. b; 2. d; 3. c; 4. d; 5. b

admire

© Carson-Dellosa

energy

© Carson-Dellosa

geometry

© Carson-Dellosa

government

© Carson-Dellosa

healthy

© Carson-Dellosa

knowledge

© Carson-Dellosa

leader

© Carson-Dellosa

passage

© Carson-Dellosa

community

© Carson-Dellosa

| opinion | material | conversion |
|---------|----------|------------|
| © Carson-Dellosa | © Carson-Dellosa | © Carson-Dellosa |

| contrast | procedure | descriptive |
|----------|-----------|-------------|
| © Carson-Dellosa | © Carson-Dellosa | © Carson-Dellosa |

| chart | transportation | fraction |
|-------|----------------|----------|
| © Carson-Dellosa | © Carson-Dellosa | © Carson-Dellosa |

temperature

© Carson-Dellosa

estimate

© Carson-Dellosa

climate

© Carson-Dellosa

subject

© Carson-Dellosa

symbol

© Carson-Dellosa

compare

© Carson-Dellosa

object

© Carson-Dellosa

system

© Carson-Dellosa

economy

© Carson-Dellosa

| sentence | verb | pronoun |
|---|---|---|
| © Carson-Dellosa | © Carson-Dellosa | © Carson-Dellosa |

| phrase | adjective | preposition |
|---|---|---|
| © Carson-Dellosa | © Carson-Dellosa | © Carson-Dellosa |

| noun | adverb | declarative |
|---|---|---|
| © Carson-Dellosa | © Carson-Dellosa | © Carson-Dellosa |

interrogative

exclamatory

imperative

contraction

?

/

/

-

—

| paragraph | future tense | predicate |
|---|---|---|
| © Carson-Dellosa | © Carson-Dellosa | © Carson-Dellosa |
| apostrophe | question mark | past tense |
| © Carson-Dellosa | © Carson-Dellosa | © Carson-Dellosa |
| exclamation point | period | comma |
| © Carson-Dellosa | © Carson-Dellosa | © Carson-Dellosa |

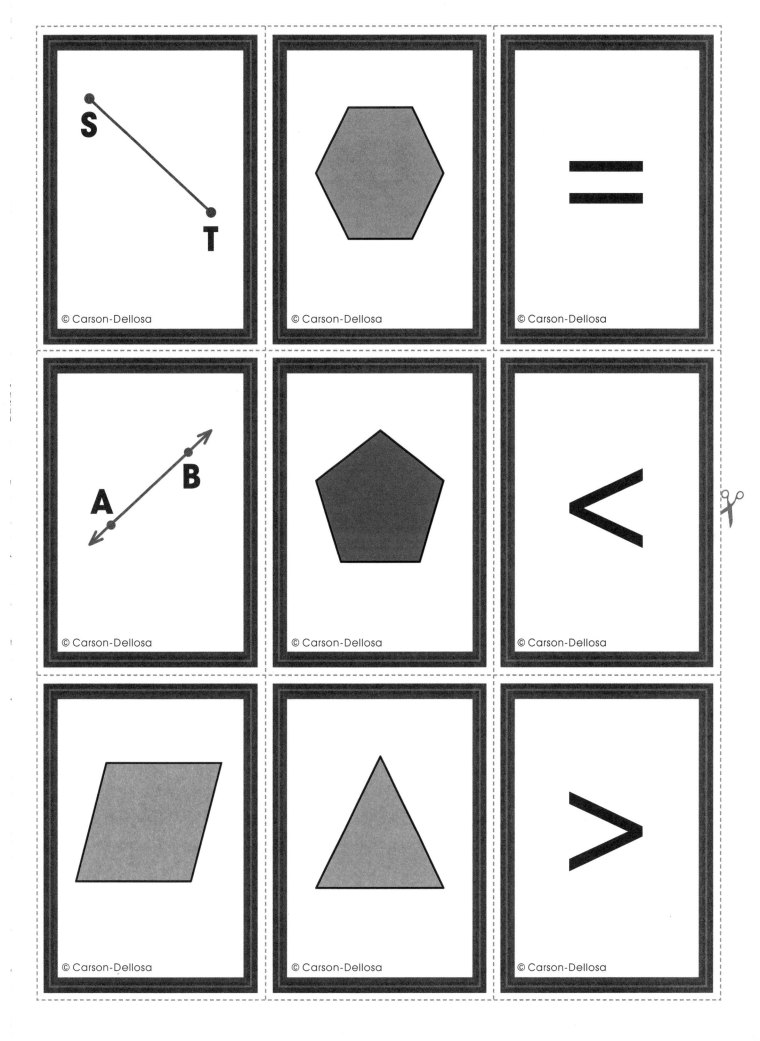

| | | |
|---|---|---|
| line segment ST | hexagon | equal to |
| © Carson-Dellosa | © Carson-Dellosa | © Carson-Dellosa |
| line AB | pentagon | less than |
| © Carson-Dellosa | © Carson-Dellosa | © Carson-Dellosa |
| parallelogram | triangle | greater than |
| © Carson-Dellosa | © Carson-Dellosa | © Carson-Dellosa |

$14\overline{)1.218}$

$24\overline{)7.28}$

$46\overline{)0.2346}$

$$4\frac{1}{3}$$
$$-2\frac{3}{8}$$

$$\frac{13}{15}$$
$$-\frac{2}{3}$$

$$\frac{3}{4}$$
$$-\frac{1}{5}$$

$$2\frac{2}{3}$$
$$-2\frac{1}{3}$$

$$4\frac{7}{10}$$
$$-1\frac{4}{5}$$

$$\frac{5}{7}$$
$$-\frac{3}{7}$$

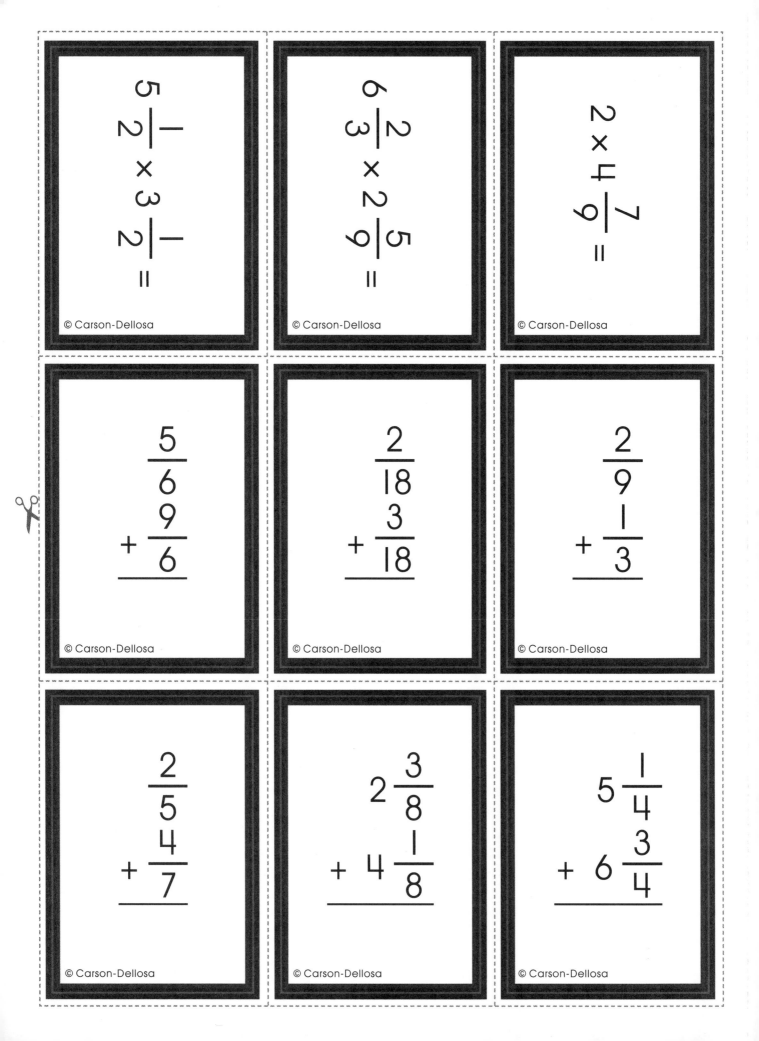

**Card 1:** $5\frac{1}{2} \times 3\frac{1}{2} =$

© Carson-Dellosa

**Card 2:** $6\frac{2}{3} \times 2\frac{5}{9} =$

© Carson-Dellosa

**Card 3:** $2 \times 4\frac{7}{9} =$

© Carson-Dellosa

**Card 4:**
$$\frac{5}{6} + \frac{1}{6}$$

© Carson-Dellosa

**Card 5:**
$$\frac{2}{18} + \frac{3}{18}$$

© Carson-Dellosa

**Card 6:**
$$\frac{2}{9} + \frac{1}{3}$$

© Carson-Dellosa

**Card 7:**
$$\frac{2}{5} + \frac{4}{7}$$

© Carson-Dellosa

**Card 8:**
$$2\frac{3}{8} + 4\frac{1}{8}$$

© Carson-Dellosa

**Card 9:**
$$5\frac{1}{4} + 6\frac{3}{4}$$

© Carson-Dellosa

```
    5,632              152            4,990
       62              455              876
       53              212              501
+     487          +   111         +    642
```
© Carson-Dellosa          © Carson-Dellosa          © Carson-Dellosa

```
    6,388            5,629            7,963
 -  5,122         -  1,453         -  5,741
```
© Carson-Dellosa          © Carson-Dellosa          © Carson-Dellosa

```
    15.2             44.2             12.3
+    2.8         +   16.3         +    1.5
```
© Carson-Dellosa          © Carson-Dellosa          © Carson-Dellosa

| 2,432 | 8,476 | 755 |
|---|---|---|
| 252 | 933 | 493 |
| 133 | 102 | 382 |
| − 48 | − 26 | − 64 |

| 7,458 | 9,466 | 12,453 |
|---|---|---|
| + 4,832 | + 5,861 | + 2,721 |

| 36.5 | 46.9 | 96.32 |
|---|---|---|
| − 5.4 | − 18.3 | − 2.05 |

| 2,586<br>× 3 | 4,209<br>× 13 | 6,015<br>× 12 |
|---|---|---|
| © Carson-Dellosa | © Carson-Dellosa | © Carson-Dellosa |
| 236<br>× 419 | 406<br>× 258 | 768<br>× 357 |
| © Carson-Dellosa | © Carson-Dellosa | © Carson-Dellosa |
| 10.2<br>× 3.6 | 0.12<br>× 0.04 | 53.3<br>× 5.2 |
| © Carson-Dellosa | © Carson-Dellosa | © Carson-Dellosa |

$6\overline{)24}$

$8\overline{)48}$

$9\overline{)108}$

$15\overline{)75}$

$5\overline{)2,145}$

$32\overline{)148}$

$$\begin{array}{r} 14.30 \\ \times\ 8.63 \\ \hline \end{array}$$

$$\begin{array}{r} 22.53 \\ \times\ 4.92 \\ \hline \end{array}$$

$$\begin{array}{r} 54.46 \\ \times\ 2.68 \\ \hline \end{array}$$

The Original
# Summer Bridge Activities™

## Congratulations!

This certifies that

_____
Name

has completed **Summer Bridge Activities**™.

_____
Parent's Signature

**www.carsondellosa.com**